NEW DIRECTIONS FOR EVALUATION
A Publication of the American Evaluation Association

Gary T. Henry, *Georgia State University*
EDITOR-IN-CHIEF

Jennifer C. Greene, *Cornell University*
EDITOR-IN-CHIEF

Creating Effective Graphs: Solutions for a Variety of Evaluation Data

Gary T. Henry
Georgia State University

EDITOR

Number 73, Spring 1997

JOSSEY-BASS PUBLISHERS
San Francisco

CREATING EFFECTIVE GRAPHS: SOLUTIONS FOR A VARIETY OF
EVALUATION DATA
Gary T. Henry (ed.)
New Directions for Evaluation, no. 73
Jennifer C. Greene, Gary T. Henry, Editors-in-Chief

Microfilm copies of issues and articles are available in 16mm and 35mm,
as well as microfiche in 105mm, through University Microfilms Inc., 300
North Zeeb Road, Ann Arbor, Michigan 48106-1346.

ISSN 0164-7989   ISBN 0-7879-9821-4

NEW DIRECTIONS FOR EVALUATION is part of The Jossey-Bass Education
Series and is published quarterly by Jossey-Bass Inc., Publishers, 350
Sansome Street, San Francisco, California 94104-1342.

Subscriptions cost $61.00 for individuals and $96.00 for institutions,
agencies, and libraries. Prices subject to change.

EDITORIAL CORRESPONDENCE should be addressed to the Editors-in-Chief,
Jennifer C. Greene, Department of Human Service Studies, Cornell University, Ithaca, NY 14853-4401, or Gary T. Henry, Public Administration
and Urban Studies, Georgia State University, Atlanta, GA 30302-4039.

Jossey-Bass Web address: http://www.josseybass.com

Manufactured in the United States of America on Lyons Falls
Turin Book. This paper is acid-free and 100 percent totally
chlorine-free.

EDITORIAL POLICY AND PROCEDURES

NEW DIRECTIONS FOR EVALUATION, a quarterly sourcebook, is an official publication of the American Evaluation Association. The journal publishes empirical, methodological, and theoretical works on all aspects of evaluation and related fields. Substantive areas may include any program, field, or issue with which evaluation is concerned, such as government performance, tax policy, energy, environment, mental health, education, job training, medicine, and public health. Also included are such topics as product evaluation, personnel evaluation, policy analysis, and technology assessment. In all cases, the focus on evaluation is more important than the substantive topics. We are particularly interested in encouraging a diversity of evaluation perspectives and experiences and in expanding the boundaries of our field beyond the evaluation of social programs.

The editors do not consider or publish unsolicited single manuscripts. Each issue of the journal is devoted to a single topic, with contributions solicited, organized, reviewed, and edited by a guest editor. Issues may take any of several forms, such as a series of related chapters, a debate, or a long article followed by brief critical commentaries. In all cases, the proposals must follow a specific format, which can be obtained from the editor-in-chief. These proposals are sent to members of the editorial board and to relevant substantive experts for peer review. The process may result in acceptance, a recommendation to revise and resubmit, or rejection. However, the editors are committed to working constructively with potential guest editors to help them develop acceptable proposals.

Jennifer C. Greene, Editor-in-Chief
Department of Human Service Studies
Cornell University
Ithaca, NY 14853-4401

Gary T. Henry, Editor-in-Chief
Public Administration and Urban Studies
Georgia State University
Atlanta, GA 30302-4039

CONTENTS

PART THREE: Displaying Trends

PART FOUR: Displaying Relationships

EDITOR'S NOTES

The idea for *Creating Effective Graphs* came when I offered workshops and presentations on the research that went into my 1995 book *Graphing Data: Techniques for Display and Analysis*. Many of those who attended would bring a graph or fax one to me later. Often the ideas were effective and well-executed solutions to particular problems that most of us face sooner or later. This sourcebook is an attempt to share these solutions with a larger audience.

This edition contains more than the average number of chapters for a *New Directions for Evaluation* sourcebook. It employs a casebook strategy to illustrate what good graphs are, how they come to be, and what they contribute to analysis and presentation in evaluations. Each author submitted one or more graphs that were effective for them in an evaluation. While we had some fun exchanging ideas and whittling and tweaking some of the displays in one way or another, the graphs maintain their real-life character.

My colleague Mike Hendricks began this project with me. He helped identify some of the authors. He reviewed some of the early graphs. We discussed many graphical ideas as the project began to take shape. Unfortunately, he was called in another direction during the project, as successful evaluators so often are. Many of his good ideas show up in the sourcebook, and I am sure he would have lent more good advice to all of us had he not been pressed into service elsewhere.

I wish to acknowledge my research assistant, Kathy Dolan, who added this to a list of evaluation-related projects we have worked on. Kathy was instrumental in pulling the sourcebook together. Another colleague, Paul Vaughn, provided insights and final touches to several of the graphs in the sourcebook, as well as alternatives that we shared with the authors for them to reflect on. Another associate, Kris Byron, provided able editorial assistance.

I also want to thank the authors. They expended considerable effort to make a graphical solution available to a wider audience after it had achieved success in its first endeavor. I trust that you will find their work as enlightening as I have.

Gary T. Henry
Editor

GARY T. HENRY is director of the Applied Research Center and associate professor in the Departments of Public Administration and Political Science in the School of Policy Studies at Georgia State University.

INTRODUCTION

Graphs are commonly used to present evaluation data. Their popularity for this and other uses stems from their ability to communicate information simply and efficiently. Graphs are powerful tools for evaluators, who must compete for their audience's time. The audience can quickly retrieve information from a graph, without technical training or a particular talent with numbers. That is, good graphs—well-composed and well-executed graphs—have these qualities. Unfortunately, getting a graph to function in these ways is sometimes an adventure. Combining data, software, and hardware to make a graph is often a tedious task. This sourcebook is an attempt to share ideas and improve the hit-or-miss nature of graphical production.

Many of the graphs in this sourcebook have an "aha!" quality. Something about the final product says to us, "That's what I would have done if I had known how to do it." The graphs are solutions to problems that arise when communicating evaluation findings. The problems are common and recurring. Sometimes they involve communicating a known finding that could be contained in a table but would be much more difficult to extract from the table (see Chapter Nine). Sometimes they expose biases in the narrative reporting of the data (see Chapter Five). Sometimes they reveal implications that would have gone unnoticed (see Chapters Eleven and Seven) and allow new findings to emerge. The graphs can be used for discovery or for presentation; they are sometimes designed for evaluators and other times for evaluation audiences.

The chapters in this sourcebook describe cases in which the authors found a graphical solution to an evaluation problem. The creative, clever solutions they offer might have been lost to most of us because they were produced for important but under-read reports. The chapters in this sourcebook describe evaluators' responses in real evaluation situations. Most show the process of getting to the final graph by showing a standard "default" graph and a final graph that was used in an actual evaluation. Each author describes the evaluation problem, the data, and the software employed for the final graph. Each chapter makes the point that graphing, like writing, is a process that requires constant revision. Just as first drafts of anything are rarely publishable, graphs must go through multiple versions before they are useable. Therefore they must be drafted early in the process and refined over multiple iterations. Deadlines and software programs that present a steep learning curve add to the temptation to stop revising too soon. The graphs in this volume may provide some needed traction.

Overview of the Contents

A few authors have for years been providing insights into the effective use of graphical data displays. Tufte's work (1983, 1990) provides important theoretical insights and principles for graphical excellence, with an emphasis on the aesthetic quality of graphs. Bertin (1983) connects graphical displays to the theories that undergird semiology, developing a complex and compelling system for using graphs as symbols. Cleveland (1995) and Wainer (1992) have invented and tested some graphical methods for many research quandaries. Tukey (1977), perhaps best known for his work in exploratory data analysis, reinvented the use of graphical methods to do serious analytical work. *Graphing Data* (Henry, 1995) represented my first attempt to synthesize the work on graphical display that simplifies the process of constructing graphs and fulfills their analytical and communication purposes. These works leave us with an additional task, the task of finding the graphical solutions that will work with particular evaluation problems.

The chapters in this sourcebook are organized into four sections, following the breakdown in *Graphing Data:*

1. Displaying Parts of the Whole
2. Displaying Identifiable Units
3. Displaying Trends
4. Displaying Relationships

These four types of displays constitute the most frequently used types of graphs. Though statistical maps are becoming more and more widely used due to geographical information systems, they are beyond the scope of this sourcebook.

In Part One, Deborah Bonnet (Chapter One) steps up the amount of data, from one example to the next, in graphs using horizontal bars. The chapter illuminates the analytical potential of the horizontal-bar format for nontechnical audiences. Helen Brown, Katharyn Marks, and Margret Straw (Chapter Two) show how a clear purpose combined with a simple format— pie and bar graphs—can quickly communicate survey results. Both Brown, Marks, and Straw and Edward Parker and Louis Mortillaro (Chapter Three) illustrate ways to handle contingent data or data that result from skip patterns, where some questions do or do not apply based on responses to earlier questions. Parker and Mortillaro make effective use of a flowchart to show results in a way that makes them easily digestible and moves the audience from asking What? to asking Why?

The chapters in Part Two deal with comparing multiple cases in situations in which it is important to be able to identify each individual case. Alvin Glymph and I (Chapter Four) show how aggregated performance data can be displayed and the impact of a phenomenon known as Simpson's paradox on the perception of the comparisons. James Sinacore (Chapter Five) discusses the use of dot charts to show how units change over time. This format avoids the mistakes that can be made when using more common formats, by displaying the amount of change in both a relative and absolute sense rather than having the reader visually estimate the differences in units at two points in time. By representing the difference with a visual symbol, Sinacore does not commit the mistake of forcing readers to draw out the difference for themselves, which can lead to inaccurate perceptions of the change (Beherens, Stock, and Sedgwick, 1991; Henry, 1993).

Part Three introduces trend graphs. Robin Turpin (Chapter Six) shows the graphical difference between comparing data (in this case, performance data for a hospital) on one performance measure and using two different measures of variability, one internal and the other external. Turpin effectively demonstrates that "less is more"—that by restricting the display to one important task, it can be done with greater clarity and purpose. Adding another task to the same graph would have rendered the graph unintelligible. Kathleen Sullivan (Chapter Seven) shows two trend displays that were effectively used in evaluation reports: one replaced bars depicting the values at specific time periods with lines and added projections; another used cohort rather than aggregate data for time periods, which allowed the evaluators to tease out an interesting relationship. Mika'il DeVeaux (Chapter Eight) uses bar and line graphs to illustrate trend data, pointing out that graphs should be tailored to the specific question and presented for a specific audience. He also emphasizes that one should never assume that an audience has statistical or graphical knowledge.

The three chapters in Part Four show relationships between variables. Using an example from criminal justice evaluations, James Derzon (Chapter Nine) graphically depicts the flow as individuals identified as "at-risk" in one period are classified as either violent or nonviolent later. Using a graph, Derzon reduces the bias in the perception of false positive and true negatives. Lois Sayrs (Chapter Ten) offers some graphical displays of pooled time series data that cast doubt on the effectiveness of an energy conservation program. Like Sinacore does in Chapter Five, Sayrs plots the change in energy use rather than the values for amount of energy use in two periods. She also packs in more information using the plotting symbols to convey more information. Barbara Starrett and Matthew Johnsen (Chapter Eleven) show an effective graph for displaying networks between organizations. The pattern is arranged to show major and minor constellations of organization, and it uses the size of the organization's plotting symbol to indicate its centrality.

Finally, in the Conclusion, I outline some of the principles that are important in preparing a good graph. Knowing the purpose, the audience, the presentation media, and the technology but first and foremost allocating enough time are important principles to be followed.

The graphs in each chapter of this sourcebook achieve their purpose of communicating some findings or other evaluation information. All are competent graphs. The authors eschew using distracting elements and trying to do too much. Graphs that try to do too much often fail to do anything. Most of the graphs presented here appear simple, even self-evident, but show a new and more complete way of looking at a finding. They are not solutions to every display problem, but they often contain an idea or a technique that can set you off in the right direction to find the solution you are looking for.

References

Beherens, J. T., Stock, W. A., and Sedgwick, C. A. "Judgment Errors in Elementary Box Plot Displays." *Communications in Statistics,* 1991, *19,* 245–262.

Bertin, J. *Seminology of Graphics: Diagrams Networks Maps* (W. J. Berg, trans.). Madison: University of Wisconsin Press, 1983. (Originally published 1967.)

Cleveland, W. S. *The Elements of Graphing Data.* Belmont, Calif.: Wadsworth, 1995.

Henry, G. T. "Using Graphical Displays for Evaluation Data." *Evaluation Review,* 1993, *17* (1), 60–78.

Henry, G. T. *Graphing Data: Techniques for Display and Analysis.* Thousand Oaks, Calif.: Sage, 1995.

Tufte, E. R. *The Visual Display of Quantitative Information.* Cheshire, Conn.: Graphics Press, 1983.

Tufte, E. R. *Envisioning Information.* Cheshire, Conn.: Graphics Press, 1990.

Tukey, J. W. *Exploratory Data Analysis.* Reading, Mass.: Addison-Wesley, 1977.

Wainer, H. "Understanding Graphics and Tables." *Educational Researcher,* 1992, *21* (1), 14–23.

GARY T. HENRY is director of the Applied Research Center and associate professor in the Departments of Public Administration and Political Science in the School of Policy Studies at Georgia State University.

PART ONE

Displaying Parts of the Whole

*Several increasingly complex examples of horizontal bar graphs are
presented to illustrate how to use multiple graphic elements to create
graphs with high information density.*

Packing It In with Horizontal Bars

Deborah G. Bonnet

If I knew how, I would set the default on my Harvard Graphics software program
to "horizontal bars." I prefer horizontal bar graphs to column bar graphs, because
they do not require readers to crane their necks. Labels are right-side-up, and
the graph is given a portrait orientation. Horizontal bar graphs also allow evaluators to pack a great deal of information into a single graph.

Clustered Bars for Two-Way Comparisons

When crosstabs are the analysis of choice, a clustered bar presentation is likely
to be in order. My firm was invited to survey nonprofit executives to find new
ways of developing alliances between colleges and nonprofits to help prepare
undergraduates for careers in youth and human services organizations. One idea
we discussed to help students find out about jobs in the nonprofit sector was
to develop a nationwide computerized job bank. In our phone survey of nonprofit executives, we asked how they currently recruit entry-level professionals.
We also asked them a series of questions about what they look for in candidates.
Then we asked them to think about the last person they hired and answer
another series of questions. Figure 1.1 shows the findings from the questions
"How did you find the person you hired?" (method used successfully) and
"How else did you locate candidates for the position?" (method used).

Since most respondents indicated that they recruited for the position
locally, the client's idea of creating a national job data bank would mean depart-
ing from a virtually universal practice. Three techniques were used to clearly
illustrate this information in a graph: (1) using a darker bar for the variable of
primary interest, in this case "Used," (2) presenting the methods in descending order by the variable of primary interest, and (3) grouping the recruitment
methods as local versus national.

New Directions for Evaluation, no. 73, Spring 1997 © Jossey-Bass Publishers

Figure 1.1. A Clustered Bar Graph Illustrating a Two-Way Comparison

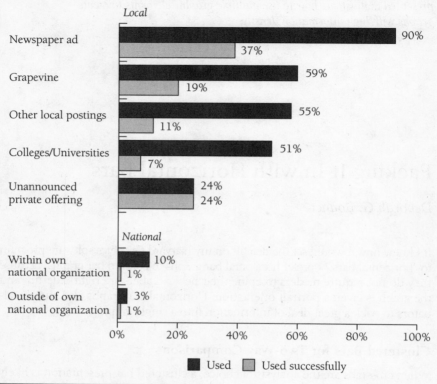

N = 100 nonprofit executives in six U.S. cities.

Used: How most recent opening was announced. *Used successfully:* How most recent hire was located.

Unless the "natural grouping" principle takes precedence, I always use descending order, since it is more visually pleasing and the order of the categories contains ranking information. (The two principles do not conflict in this case, but it seems that they usually do.)

This study also looked at which recruitment methods have the highest success rates, which is of interest to both employers and job seekers. Employers can find out which methods will most likely result in hires and more quickly fill vacancies. Job seekers can find out which methods to use by looking at which ones are most likely to result in hires. The employer's question is answered by comparing the dark bars to the light bars. It is fairly easy to see that most employers believe that newspaper ads and the grapevine are the two most effective recruitment methods. In addition, this graph provides the reader sufficient data to calculate the success ratio of each recruitment method, if he or she is so inclined. Job seekers need only look at the "used successfully" data to know what to do—namely, bypass the campus placement office, live where they want to work, and unless they know someone, buy a newspaper.

The clustered-bar graphing style also works well when each item stands alone and the main point is to compare across groups or time periods.

Stacked Bars for Ordinal Data

If cumulative frequencies are the most interesting thing on the printout, use stacked bars.

Though I personally avoid asking people to rank-order things, a colleague who calls upon my graphical assistance likes using this method. We have, at least, landed on a presentation style that works. Figure 1.2 is from a recent study in which PSL & Associates followed up participants of an intensive two-year leadership education program offered ten years ago. The client had a good sense going into the evaluation that the program had been successful, in that participants had, indeed, gone forth and done good work on behalf of Indiana's youth. Since the program was also quite expensive, one purpose of the study was to single out the key contributing factors of its success. One item on the mail survey asked participants to reflect on that topic. They were to select and rank-order the five most significant program features from a list of nine (the ones shown on the graph). The first version of this graph displayed all five rankings, but we discovered that showing just the top three rankings made the same point more simply.

The advantage of stacked bars is that they allow readers to set their own standards. This graph, for example, could spawn the argument that the program's most valued feature was not its involvement of national experts but its focus on personal growth, since that feature drew the most number 1 rankings. The important thing to keep in mind with stacked bars is to make sure the categories are properly ordered, with the highest rating or most important data point next to the axis. This allows readers to easily compare across items on that criterion.

Paired Stacked Bars for Scaled Data with an Underlying Dichotomy

If someone is counting the yeas and the nays, use both sides of the axis. Figure 1.3 presents the results of a standard end-of-session participant evaluation form, designed by the client and employing a five-point rating scale. All five response categories are illustrated through shading in the expected sequence from bad (black) to good (white), with "satisfied" customers shown on the right of the axis and "disappointed" ones on the left. In keeping with the principle of placing the most extreme or interesting category next to the axis, the highest ratings are just to the right of the axis and the lowest just to the left. This leaves everything in a rather unusual order, one that admittedly takes some getting used to. I have found that people do catch on and like this format once they see how well it indicates strengths and weaknesses.

Figure 1.2. A Stacked Bar Graph Displaying Ordinal Data

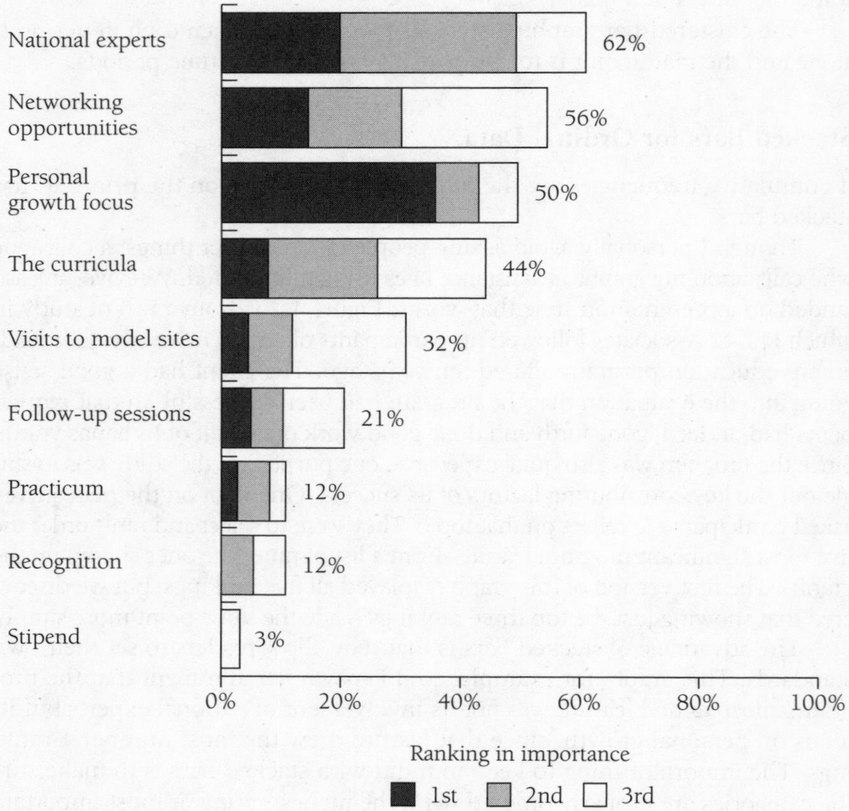

N = 34 graduates, ten years later.

This time I counted the "fair" (middle) rating as negative, which is perhaps uncharitable of me. Usually I leave out neutral ratings and missing data from graphs in this format, though I do count them in the percentage base.

Paired Bars for Triangulation

If you measured more or less the same thing in two different ways, give the reader a break and put those measurements on the same page.

Indiana United Ways have received financial and technical assistance since 1991 through a capacity-building initiative supported by the Lilly Endowment. A key element of the program's internal evaluation is a self-assessment instrument to be completed by consensus of United Way's boards of directors and staff. The instrument has 140 items in eighteen subscales grouped in five areas

Figure 1.3. A Paired Stacked Bar Graph Showing Scaled Data with an Underlying Dichotomy

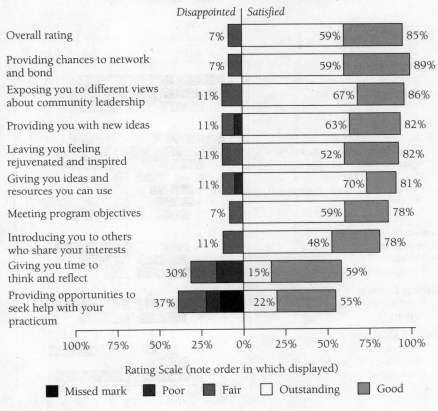

Disappointed | Satisfied

	Disappointed	Satisfied
Overall rating	7%	59% ... 85%
Providing chances to network and bond	7%	59% ... 89%
Exposing you to different views about community leadership	11%	67% ... 86%
Providing you with new ideas	11%	63% ... 82%
Leaving you feeling rejuvenated and inspired	11%	52% ... 82%
Giving you ideas and resources you can use	11%	70% ... 81%
Meeting program objectives	7%	59% ... 78%
Introducing you to others who share your interests	11%	48% ... 78%
Giving you time to think and reflect	30%	15% ... 59%
Providing opportunities to seek help with your practicum	37%	22% ... 55%

100%   75%   50%   25%   0%   25%   50%   75%   100%

Rating Scale (note order in which displayed)

■ Missed mark   ■ Poor   ■ Fair   □ Outstanding   ■ Good

N = 27 (87 percent of 31 participants)

Percentages based on all surveys submitted; blank responses are not shown.

corresponding to the program's theory of capacity building. Figure 1.4 summarizes the 1992 and 1995 assessments of participating United Ways as they reflect recent gains in organizational capacities.

On the left side of the graph are straightforward frequencies of response to the direct question of how United Ways rate their progress (or backsliding) over the past year, with only positive responses displayed. On the right side is the mean gain between 1992 and 1995 on subscale scores converted to one-hundred-point scales. The latter measure is not only more subtle than the former but also refers to a three-year rather than one-year period. Nevertheless, the two measures are correlated, not only from United Way to United Way but (to a lesser extent) from subscale to subscale. The measures are convergent to the extent that the left and right profiles mirror one another.

Figure 1.4. A Paired Bar Graph with Triangulation

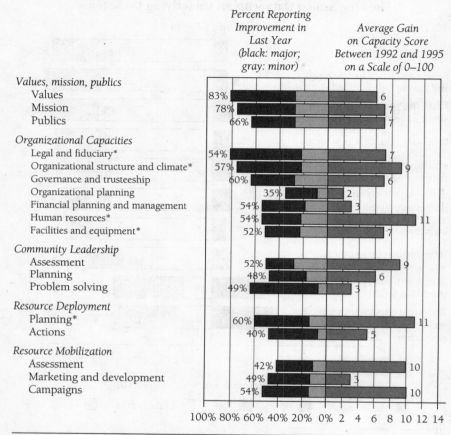

35 United Ways responding in 1995 (left); 26 responding in 1992 and 1995 (right)

*Gain (indicated by bar on right side of chart) is statistically significant.

Another way to illustrate convergence is to put several simple graphs with the same x-axis variable on the same page. This works especially well with time series data presented vertically. This allows you to illustrate the effects of several independent variables on the dependent variable.

Conclusion

Of course, the fact that it is possible to squeeze a lot of information into a graph does not necessarily make it a good idea to do so. I, for one, have been known to get carried away with this—perhaps, one might argue, on these very pages. A sure sign of excess is when the graph becomes less accessible than the table it was intended to replace. Another is when you pick up your own graph six months later and it takes more than half a minute to figure it out.

Each of the examples presented above was for an audience with relatively high stakes in the findings. The graphics appeared in written reports, and the primary users were briefed in person. It was reasonable to expect them to spend several minutes studying each graph and several more discussing them with colleagues. Under other circumstances, such as when the audience is less motivated, when the purpose is more to persuade than to inform, or when a sound bite is all you can get, something simpler would be a better idea.

DEBORAH G. BONNET has been an evaluation consultant since 1974. She currently heads D. Bonnet Associates in Indianapolis.

Describes a means of translating data from multipart survey items into information a diverse audience can use for effective program planning and implementation.

Use of Graphics to Illustrate Responses to Multipart Survey Items

Helen Brown, Katharyn Marks, Margret Straw

The American Association of Retired Persons (AARP) is a nonprofit membership association that provides services to and advocates for older adults. Volunteers implement many of the association's programs and advocacy activities, in collaboration with paid staff. When we evaluate AARP's volunteer programs, we routinely communicate the findings to a very broad audience, ranging from the volunteers and staff who deliver the programs to program managers and senior executives with oversight responsibilities. Graphics have been an invaluable tool for describing and summarizing large amounts of quantitative information to these varied audiences.

This chapter describes graphics used in two AARP studies. In both cases, the graphs illustrated key findings from multipart survey questions. They appeared in written reports intended for the broad audience described above. The first study was an evaluation of AARP VOTE, the association's voter education program. The second assessed awareness of AARP's community-level programs and activities. The specific problems that were addressed and the evolution of the graphs are discussed separately for each study.

AARP VOTE

AARP VOTE has two primary objectives: to provide the public with nonpartisan information on issues of interest to older adults and to inform elected officials and candidates of AARP's positions on key policy issues. The graph we

Note: The views presented herein are those of the authors and do not necessarily represent the policies or viewpoints of the American Association of Retired Persons.

created focused on one key indicator of success for the program—whether officials and candidates said information about AARP's positions had an impact on their position on issues. The data used in the graph came from a telephone survey of U.S. senators elected in 1992, incumbents and challengers for the 1994 U.S. Senate and House races, or their proxies (chiefs of staff or administrative aides). A total of 294 interviews were completed of 567 attempted.

The graph illustrates responses to a two-part question. First the respondents were asked, "After learning or reading about AARP's positions on the issues, do you feel your position grew closer to AARP's, or did it have no effect?" The response categories for this question were (1) no effect, (2) grew closer, and (3) don't know. Those who answered "no effect" were asked a follow-up question: "Which of the following best describes why AARP's information had no effect on your issue positions?" The response categories for this question were as follows:

1. It had no effect because (the candidate) is already in agreement with AARP.
2. It had no effect because AARP was not persuasive.
3. It had no effect because AARP's positions were not well communicated.

Although not offered as a choice, "don't know" was coded when respondents volunteered that answer.

Data were analyzed using the Statistical Package for the Social Sciences (SPSS) for Windows. The percent of responses in each category were computed using the frequencies command in SPSS and were graphed using Harvard Graphics for Windows.

The Original Graph. The original approach to graphing these questions was to produce two pie charts (see Figure 2.1). Because the linked pie feature produced overlapping labels, two separate pie charts were created and then cut-and-pasted to the same page. The pie on the left presented the data from the primary question on the impact of AARP, while the pie on the right was used for the follow-up question on the reason for a lack of impact. Shades of gray were used to distinguish among and call attention to different slices.

The Revised Graph. The revised graph, shown in Figure 2.2, is a linked pie and bar graph that was created by selecting that option in Harvard Graphics for Windows. The pie continues to represent responses to the lead question. It is now rotated so that the "no effect" slice faces the bar. The bar represents the follow-up question. It illustrates all of the reasons for the lack of effect and is visibly linked to the "no effect" slice of the pie. Shades of gray have been replaced by patterns throughout.

We revised the graph for several reasons. First, and most importantly, we wanted to better communicate the findings. We wanted the reader to understand that candidates' views moved closer to AARP's position almost four in ten times (39 percent) and that when AARP had no effect, it was often because the candidate already agreed with the association's position (45 percent of the time). We also wanted the reader to quickly grasp the reasons for a lack of effect that could be addressed programmatically (for example, poor communication).

Figure 2.1. Original Graph for AARP VOTE

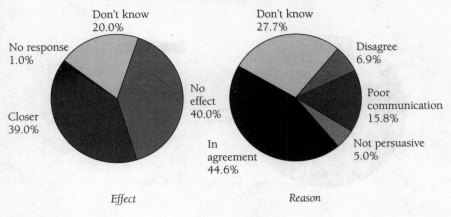

Effect   Reason

N = 153

The original graph emphasized the lack of effect without clearly indicating that this lack was not always negative. Thus it tended to distort the findings. This is one of the significant graphing problems Tufte discusses (1989). The linking in the revised graph addressed this problem. Figure 2.2 clearly indicates that the "no effect" response occurs for a variety of reasons, some positive and some negative.

Second, the original graph did not clearly indicate that the pie on the right represented the responses to a follow-up question that was asked only of those who said contacts by AARP VOTE had no effect. The revised graph makes this clear by visually linking a single slice of the pie to the bar giving reasons for no effect.

Third, we wished to improve the visual presentation. Using shades of gray for the pie slices was very effective in the original, but it made the graphs vulnerable to degeneration of gray in photocopying. Thus, patterns were substituted as a way of highlighting the differences in the proportions for each response category. Although bar graphs are usually ordered by size, this resulted in text overlaps, because there was not enough space for the text for small segments of the bar (Roth and Mattis, 1995). The bar was reordered to overcome that problem.

AARP Awareness Study

AARP's annual awareness study measures awareness of the association and its programs, services, and activities. In 1994, study data were collected in telephone interviews with a national random sample of 2,003 adults age forty or older. Included in the sample were respondents who either expressed an unaided recollection of AARP or recognized the association's name when

Figure 2.2. Revised Graph for AARP VOTE

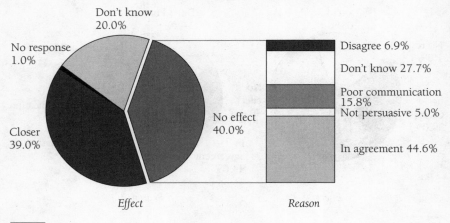

Don't know
20.0%

No response
1.0%

Closer
39.0%

No effect
40.0%

Disagree 6.9%

Don't know 27.7%

Poor communication
15.8%
Not persuasive 5.0%

In agreement 44.6%

Effect   *Reason*

$N = 153$

prompted with it. Data for the study were weighted to reflect the 1990 census data parameters for age, race, and sex.

At the time of the study, the association had nine area offices with responsibility for publicizing and managing AARP's community programs and delivering various services. These offices might emphasize or highlight different programs in a given year, but each was responsible for providing some level of service across all program areas.

The Area 8 awareness graph was prepared as a supplement to the national report on the study. It specifically sought to help AARP's Area 8 staff see where their area differed from national results on the levels of awareness of AARP's programs and activities. The levels of awareness were measured through closed-ended questions that provided activity descriptions as cues for aided recognition.

The Original Graph. Initially, the data were presented in a horizontal bar graph produced using Harvard Graphics for Windows (see Figure 2.3). In the original graph, there are two bars for each AARP activity, one that shows the percentage of respondents from Area 8 that were aware of the activity, and another that shows awareness of that activity nationally. Since eighteen activities were explored in the survey, the graph has thirty-six bars. To know the percentage differences for the two levels, readers have to do the arithmetic themselves. The original graph also looks very cluttered and does not indicate which, if any, of the differences are statistically significant. Yet, it was important to include all eighteen activities in the same graph, because they provide context for one another.

The Revised Graph. Figure 2.4 shows the revised horizontal bar graph, which displays only one bar per activity. In this version—also prepared using Harvard Graphics for Windows—the graph displays the differences between the Area 8 and national percentages rather than providing the specific percentages

Figure 2.3. Original Graph for AARP Awareness Study

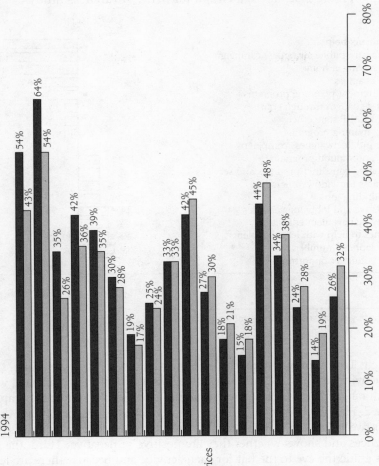

1994

Category	Black bar	Gray bar
Income tax help	54%	43%
Health care public awareness campaign	64%	54%
Help staying at home	35%	26%
Local chapters	42%	36%
Preretirement planning programs	39%	35%
Making changes through courts	30%	28%
Staffed AARP state office	19%	17%
Driver training programs	25%	24%
Other public awareness campaigns	33%	33%
Health promotion programs	42%	45%
Evaluating consumer products and services	27%	30%
Programs for widowed persons	18%	21%
Help finding jobs	15%	18%
Legislative and lobbying activities	44%	48%
Money management education	34%	38%
Hotlines to help with legal problems	24%	28%
800 telephone number	14%	19%
Local volunteer opportunities	26%	32%

Figure 2.4. Revised Graph for AARP Awareness Study

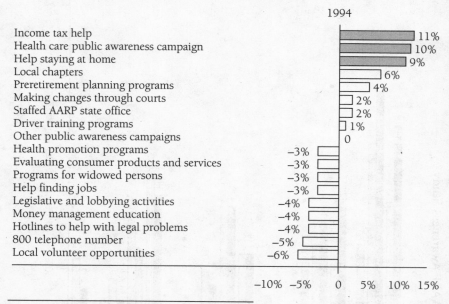

1994

Income tax help	11%
Health care public awareness campaign	10%
Help staying at home	9%
Local chapters	6%
Preretirement planning programs	4%
Making changes through courts	2%
Staffed AARP state office	2%
Driver training programs	1%
Other public awareness campaigns	0
Health promotion programs	−3%
Evaluating consumer products and services	−3%
Programs for widowed persons	−3%
Help finding jobs	−3%
Legislative and lobbying activities	−4%
Money management education	−4%
Hotlines to help with legal problems	−4%
800 telephone number	−5%
Local volunteer opportunities	−6%

−10% −5%   0   5%   10% 15%

Note: Shading denotes a statistically significant difference.

for each. This improves upon the original graph in several ways. First, since each activity now has one rather than two bars, the clutter is eliminated, while the full range of activities of interest are retained. Second, while the graph in Figure 2.3 left the reader with the burden of calculating the percentage difference between Area 8 and the national sample, the revised graph represents these differences and shows whether they are positive or negative. Third, the grid marks guide the eye to the bar for each activity, and because there are fewer bars, the shading to show the statistically significant difference is obvious.

Further, one purpose of evaluation is to identify both successes and opportunities for improvement. Here, by showing where Area 8's performance deviated positively from the national average, the graph highlights activities that could be viewed as successes (particularly those with statistically significant positive differences). Similarly, the graph identifies activities whose lower-than-average awareness levels provide opportunities for improvement. Even for those areas with differences that are not statistically significant, the size of the bars may help provide a guide for which activities need to be given priority.

Conclusion

In both cases, the revisions were driven by the need to share a complicated finding to a multipart question in a simple way. Since a primary use for each report was program planning and modification, both graphs attempted to show where the respective programs had been successful and where they clearly had room for improvement.

Both of the original graphs reflected this approach to graphing: "How can we illustrate the answers people gave to these questions?" The final graphs emerged when we changed our question to this: "What do we really want the reader to know about these findings?" In the AARP VOTE example, we wanted to combine information on success in achieving an outcome with practical information about how to improve upon their success. In the Area 8 report, we wanted staff to understand how their area or region compared with the rest of the country. Once we clarified the communication goals, the graphs emerged naturally.

The development of these graphs also reemphasized a number of other practical considerations in graphing. When creating a graph, it is very important to consider the way in which the final graph will be shared. If a graph will be included in a report that will be reproduced by photocopying, it is critical to examine the graph not only in its original state but also as it appears after being copied. Graphs done in color for presentations will probably not be suitable for reproduction in black and white. Even graphs done in shades of gray may be problematic to reproduce. The use of patterns or very simple fills helps ensure that graphs will reproduce well.

If patterns are being used as fill, the results will differ depending on the print density. Surprisingly, some patterns printed with the printer set at a high density (600 dpi) are more difficult to see than those printed at a lower density (300 dpi). In addition, because some patterns printed at a lower density have coarser lines and are more pronounced, they may make better copies than those printed at high density with very fine lines. Experimentation is critical, since what you see on the screen may not be what you get when the graph is printed and reproduced.

If multiple graphs are to be used in a document, decisions about features such as font, frame type, and fills should be made early so that all of the graphs will be uniform. This is especially important because placing graphs in a document can be very time-consuming, even in a Windows environment. The memory available in your printer and on your PC may dictate some graphing decisions. For example, printer memory will determine the size of the graph you can print and whether a graph can appear on the same page. Complicated fill patterns can take larger amounts of disk space, require more memory to print properly, and take longer to print than simple patterns (Training Resources and Data Exchange Performance-Based Management Special Interest Group, 1995).

References

Roth, S. F., and Mattis, J. "Data Characterization for the Intelligent Graphics Presentation." [http://parsys.cs.cmu.edu:80/Web/Groups/sage/DataCharacterization/DataCharacterization.html]. December 1995.

Training Resources and Data Exchange Performance-Based Management Special Interest Group. "How to Measure Performance: A Handbook of Techniques and Tools." [http://www.llnl.gov:80/PBM/handbook]. 1995.

Tufte, E. R. The Visual Display of Quantitative Information. Cheshire, Conn.: Graphics Press, 1989.

HELEN BROWN is currently senior research associate with the Evaluation Research Services Department at the American Association of Retired Persons.

KATHARYN MARKS is senior research advisor with the Evaluation Research Services Department at the American Association of Retired Persons.

MARGRET STRAW is director of the Evaluation Research Services Department at the American Association of Retired Persons.

The data presented in the table and flowcharts presented in this chapter convey the same information, but the flowchart more effectively guides the reader through the various relationships those data describe.

Graphical Presentation of Multilevel Data: Table Versus Flowchart Format

Edward A. Parker, Louis J. Mortillaro

This chapter offers a method for succinctly presenting multilevel outcomes in a single graph. To illustrate this method, we refer to an evaluation we conducted of a job training program, in which we measured the program's completion rate and the job retention rates of those who completed it. The sample consisted of 244 people who had participated in the program over a four-year period. Thus, the graph needed to focus on the participants as they moved through the program. That is, it had to display the number who left before completing the curriculum, the number who completed the curriculum and either obtained or did not obtain employment, and finally, the job retention rates for those who completed the program.

This information was particularly important to the director of the program and the agency that funded it. The data were used to determine if there were any aspects of the program that did not work or did not achieve program goals, thereby allowing necessary changes and modifications to be made (Sullivan, 1992). Consequently, the data needed to be presented in an easy-to-understand format to facilitate discussion between the funding agency and the program director about the usefulness, success, and direction of the program.

Our Approach to the Problem

Many software packages allow users to create publication-quality technical and statistical graphics. For our purposes, SPSS/PC+ 5.0 was used to correlate and analyze the data. Microsoft Word 6.0 was used to create the table (Table 3.1) and Harvard Graphics 3.0 to create the graphics (Figures 3.1 and 3.2). All software was Windows 3.11 compatible, which allowed easy movement between programs when needed.

Before deciding to display these data using a flowchart, we considered several options. Some, such as bar or pie charts, were immediately dismissed as impractical for this graphic due to the multileveled nature of the data. The data included information regarding the job status of participants thirty to ninety days after completing the program and the reasons other participants failed to complete the program. We would have needed several pie or bar graphs to include all the data. Consequently, we opted to try using a table, reproduced here in Table 3.1.

The original table accurately presented all of the information in a concise and simple manner. Nevertheless, we felt that this method left much to be desired. It did little to guide readers through the various relationships contained in the frequencies and percentages. Readers could find specific information quickly (for example, the percentage of people terminated from the program for any specific reason) but could not get a sense of the complete picture.

The table format provided useful information, but without a sense of the relationship between the observed values. For example, the first two columns appear unrelated without a closer look at the column headings. They are actually categories of the same group—those who completed the program (in contrast to those, in the third column, who did not). The table method seemed inadequate for giving the reader a clear sense of the distribution and direction

Table 3.1. The Original Data Presentation Format

	Completed Program and Got a Job	Completed Program but Did Not Get a Job	Did Not Complete Program
At 30–90 day follow-up			
Same job	94 (39%)		
New job	4 (2%)		
Unknown	35 (14%)	10 (4%)	
Reasons for termination			21 (9%)
Administrative separation			19 (7%)
Exceeded program duration			14 (6%)
Refused to continue			12 (5%)
Unable to locate			2 (1%)
Did not complete basic skills			33 (13%)
Miscellaneous			
Totals	133 (55%)	10 (4%)	101 (41%)

Total cases n = 244

of the flow of the data. Overall, the table did not allow readers to easily inter-pret the information (Edlefsen and Mauer, 1993).

Another notable, though less catastrophic, deficiency of the table was its general appearance. Though aesthetics is not the key issue in deciding which type of display is most suitable, it should not be downplayed (Hartwig and Dearing, 1993). Aesthetics influence how readers' eyes are drawn to various parts of a presentation.

The combination of these shortcomings led us to reject the table and instead use a flowchart.

The Advantages of Using a Flowchart

One of the first things one sees when looking at a flowchart is how the parts of the diagram relate to one another and to the whole (see Figure 3.1). This feature solved one of the problems we faced when using the table. By first depicting the total number of cases (244) at the top of the page and then split-ting this box into the two central categories ("Completed program" and "Did not complete program"), we established both the source and direction of the flow of the data. The lines connecting the boxes to each other and to the sub-ordinate levels of data further enhance this visual display and simplify the interpretation. The subdivision allows a clear understanding of how the sub-groups fit into the whole.

Figure 3.1. The First Flowchart

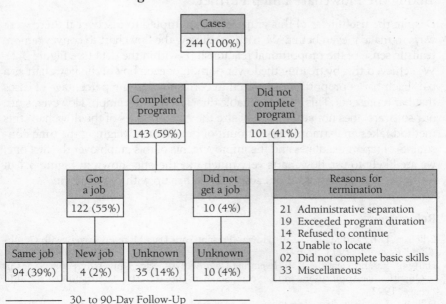

This graphical format also allows readers to visually interpret the relationships between various subgroups. Despite the relative proximity of one box, or subgroup, to another, the connecting lines clearly and unmistakably establish all pertinent relationships. With one perusal of the graph, readers can immediately and easily understand a good deal about the completion rate and placement success of this job training program.

This chart was included in a report on the job training program that was presented to the director of the program and the director of the funding agency. It produced several positive results. First, it succinctly presented answers to important questions, such as the percentage of clients who completed the program and got a job. The clear and concise format of the graphic facilitated discussion about the program's deficiencies. These are some of the questions that were raised:

• How can the attrition rate be lowered?
• Why is there so much missing follow-up data?
• What additional information would be helpful?

These questions, prompted by the increased understanding of the data, led the program director to make specific changes in his data collection processes to remedy the problem of missing follow-up data. Thus the graph achieved its purpose, which was to provide useful information in an easily understood format.

Taking the Flowchart a Step Further

Despite the usefulness of this graphic, we attempted to discover if there were ways to make it even better. We tried modifying the flowchart to convey a more realistic sense of the proportional relationships within the data (see Figure 3.2). We achieved this by treating the lower portion of each box of the flowchart as a bar. Each bar is proportionately sized to correspond to the percentage of cases that bar represents. This adds a valuable dimension to the graph. However, since our software does not automatically size the bars or boxes of the flowchart, this method takes an extraordinary amount of time. Thus, weighing the time constraints of report deadlines and the improvements of this graph over the first one, we are likely to use flowcharts very much like the one shown in Figure 3.1 in future reports, at least until our software catches up with our creativity.

References

Edlefsen, L. E., and Mauer, C. A. "How to Present Your Data More Effectively with Graphics." *Keywords,* 1993, *52,* 6–7.

Hartwig, F., and Dearing, B. E. *Exploring Data Analysis.* Sage University Paper Series in Quantitative Applications in the Social Sciences, no. 07–016. Thousand Oaks, Calif.: Sage, 1993.

Sullivan, T. J. *Applied Sociology.* New York: Macmillan, 1992.

Figure 3.2. The Revised Flowchart

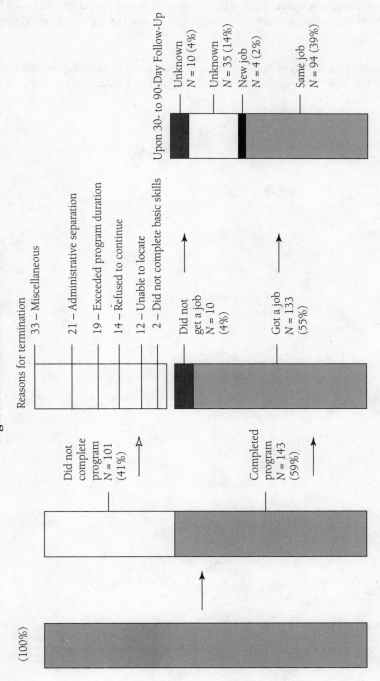

Reasons for termination

33 – Miscellaneous
21 – Administrative separation
19 – Exceeded program duration
14 – Refused to continue
12 – Unable to locate
2 – Did not complete basic skills

(100%)

Did not complete program
N = 101 (41%)

Completed program
N = 143 (59%)

Did not get a job
N = 10 (4%)

Got a job
N = 133 (55%)

Upon 30- to 90-Day Follow-Up

Unknown
N = 10 (4%)

Unknown
N = 35 (14%)

New job
N = 4 (2%)

Same job
N = 94 (39%)

EDWARD A. PARKER is a data analyst for Philliber Research Associates and is affiliated with the Department of Sociology at the State University of New York, College at New Paltz.

LOUIS J. MORTILLARO is affiliated with the Department of Sociology at the State University of New York, College at New Paltz, and is a data analyst at Philliber Research Associates.

PART TWO

Displaying Identifiable Units

When analyzing and graphing data, evaluators need to be aware of Simpson's paradox to avoid incorrect interpretations of the data.

Comparing Performance: Simpson's Paradox and Analyzing Outcomes

Alvin Glymph, Gary T. Henry

Evaluators often need to show comparisons of several units, usually naturally occurring groups such as work groups, counties, or schools, on the same measure. When used properly, graphs of this data can be used as the focus of a study or as a supplement to a study. However, some methods of graphing can lead to misinterpretations of data. We will illustrate how to accurately graph aggregate comparisons and avoid misrepresenting the data.

As an example, we present state-by-state educational performance data that were used to establish a context for understanding the educational performance of one state, Georgia. We wanted to know how Georgia compared to the rest of the nation. These comparisons were designed to allow the readers to identify the states. Though controversial, exploring differences in educational performance, with the proper use of graphs, can bring comparisons into sharp focus. However, it is very common for evaluators to simply use the aggregate scores to compare units from the secondary data, which leads to assumptions about the reasons that performance differences exist between units. Flawed assumptions frequently occur with aggregate comparisons. One major problem for interpretation, known as Simpson's paradox, is explored in this chapter.

Problem Statement

Figure 4.1 displays the 1994 National Assessment for Educational Progress (NAEP) average reading scores for the thirty-nine states that participated in the assessment, which was conducted by the National Center for Education Statistics (NCES). It allows a comparison between Georgia and the other states.

New Directions for Evaluation, no. 73, Spring 1997 © Jossey-Bass Publishers

The graph was included in two reports: the 1995 report of the Council for School Performance on education performance in Georgia (Henry and others, 1995), and a policy paper that explored reporting educational performance indicators by race (Henry and Glymph, 1995). An improvement over traditional methods of examining states' educational achievement, it helped illustrate the magnitude of the differences in educational performance between states. Not surprisingly, the graph illustrated that the educational system in the United States does not serve all students equally well.

Figure 4.1 displays the average score for each state on the 1994 NAEP fourth-grade reading assessment. It focuses on comparing the state of Georgia to the other states. This graph was constructed using Microsoft Word 6.0 and Adobe PageMaker 6.0. The NAEP scores were graphed from a base of zero to make the length of the bar representative of the score. It was tempting to graph the data on a vertical axis that begins with 180, but this would have distorted the data and overemphasized the differences (Tufte, 1983; Henry, 1995). The graph is arranged in descending order so that the states with the highest scores,

**Figure 4.1. Graph Depicting 1994
Fourth-Grade Reading Results from the NAEP**

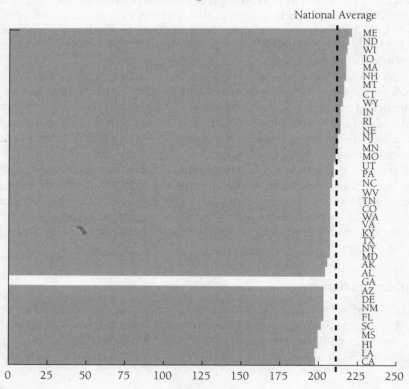

Maine, North Dakota, and Wisconsin, are on top and the lowest-performing states are at the bottom. Thus, the order of the states conveys information, and according to Bertin (1983), the image is thus easier to retain. We eliminated the space between bars to enhance the reader's ability to form an image of the data and avoid the moiré effect that thirty-nine individual, separate bars would have created. Each bar is labeled at the business end of the bar to reduce the effort required to identify any particular state's score. Finally, we added the national average as a vertical line, cutting through the bars, to allow an easy assessment of the magnitude of deviation from the average for each state.

Georgia's performance, graphed by a white bar, clearly falls below the national average. Georgia's average score is actually thirtieth out of the thirty-nine states that participated in the assessment. Georgia's ranking is not as informative as it may seem. The graph in Figure 4.1 allows the audience to visually interpret the ranking rather than simply being informed of it. Since Georgia's average is 208 and the national average is 213, the difference is less than 3 percent. Using a test of statistical differences, NAEP statisticians have determined that Georgia's score is not significantly different from the twenty-five other states in the middle of the pack (National Center for Education Statistics, 1995). We believe the graph gives an accurate impression of the magnitude of overall state differences, but we noticed something interesting. The average score cuts across the country almost like the Mason-Dixon line that geographically separates north from south. Knowing this, we should ask, Does this graph offer an accurate picture of Georgia's educational performance? Is there other information that would shed light on Georgia's performance?

Simpson's paradox warns that interpretations of overall averages can be misleading if the subgroups are of unequal proportions and averages of the subgroups are unequal on the measure being examined (Simpson, 1951). Wainer (1986) offers two methods to avoid misleading interpretations from this paradox:

1. Emphasize the disaggregated comparisons (that is, compare the subgroups).
2. Weight the disaggregated data to equal proportions, and reaggregate the data for comparative purposes (essentially, create a weighted average).

Graphics can be effectively used to illustrate the phenomenon behind Simpson's paradox to audiences that are not mathematically inclined, without losing either the ranking of the overall scores or the credibility of the evaluator in the process.

Other studies have examined gaps between African American and white student performance (Beckford and Cooley, 1993). However, we have little information about practices and programs that reduce gaps. As Corcoran and Goertz (1995) stated in their review of research on educational reform, "Our knowledge about what works under different conditions with different types of students is limited" (p. 27). Our base of knowledge pertaining to reducing racial gaps in educational performance is constrained by our reliance on aggregated information. One plausible explanation of this reliance is the fear of discussing race. Putting aside these fears, we created Figure 4.1 to allow a better understanding of educational performance and explore performance differences in the South. In addition, we used this graph to raise the salience of race in considering and comparing educational performance.

Although the subpar performance of southern states on educational measures is not surprising to many, it begs further exploration. Since Georgia's overall score is below the national average, one would assume that the average score of Georgia's African American students would fall below the national average of African Americans and that the average score of Georgia's white students would also fall below the national average of their peers. However, Table 4.1, which compares Georgia scores for African American students, white students, and overall averages for three NAEP assessments for which state-level data have been produced, displays results that contradict this assumption.

According to the 1992 NAEP reports, Georgia's African American students scored above the national average of African Americans on all three tests. For example, African American eighth graders' average math proficiency score was 241 in Georgia, compared to 236 nationally. The overall score for Georgia ranked below the national average, thirty-third of the forty-three states in which the exams were administered. However, Georgia's gap score for this assessment, or the difference between white and African American students, was twenty-nine, or eleven points lower than the average gap nationally (National Center for Education Statistics, 1993). African American students in Georgia scored above the national average for African Americans, while white students in Georgia scored below the national average. This was only evident when the scores were disaggregated by race. The relatively high performance of African Americans and the existence of the gap is lost in displays such as the one in Figure 4.1.

Simpson's paradox suggests that one argument against merely examining aggregated data is that it does not provide a picture of underlying subgroup differences that may alter performance interpretations. States' performance assessments, which are presented as overall averages, are influenced by both the *performance* and the *proportion* of African American and white students within the states. For the 1992 NAEP fourth-grade assessment, states whose

Table 4.1. Georgia and U.S. NAEP Scores, 1992

	4th grade GA Reading	4th grade US Reading	4th grade GA Math	4th grade US Math	8th grade GA Math	8th grade US Math
Overall average	213	216	214	217	259	266
African American	196	192	195	191	241	236
White	225	224	228	226	270	276
Gap	29	32	33	35	29	40

performance was below the national average were also states with larger minority populations. Above the national average, the minority population in the median state was 6.2 percent; below the national average, the minority population was 24.4 percent in the median state. Using overall averages brings one precipitously close to labeling states with high proportions of minorities as educationally inferior without regard to the performance of the minority groups within each state.

From three prior NAEP assessments, we concluded that a gap existed between African American and white student performance. We also knew that a larger concentration of African American students attend public schools in Georgia than in most other states. Figure 4.2 shows the average African American score, the average white score, and the gap between the two for all participating states for the 1994 fourth-grade mathematics assessment. Rather than relying on bars to represent the two scores, the graph uses the dot chart format (Cleveland, 1984), which allows scores to be plotted on one line, visually illustrating the gap as the distance between the two points. The display has been ordered by the overall average score for the states. Some of the states with the highest overall averages appear to have the largest gaps, as represented by the length of the line. Once again, we highlighted Georgia's scores by filling in the symbols for white and African American averages. As one can easily see from the alignment of the national averages for white and African American students with Georgia's averages, Georgia is average for both groups but below average when the group performances are aggregated. In extreme cases, both subgroup averages can exceed the national averages for the subgroups, while the aggregate average falls below the national average. Obviously, one cannot assume how well either African Americans or white students are served by an educational system by merely looking at overall averages.

Use of the Information

Our use of the two graphs in the policy report and our demonstration of the effects of Simpson's paradox led the Council for School Performance to conclude that its school performance indicators should be reported by race. The council recognized that the state must improve its performance levels, which were average by national standards, and reduce the gap between African American and white scores. Two graphs were necessary to make the point. The first graph, Figure 4.1, made Georgia's educational performance relative to the nation clear. The second, Figure 4.2, helped explain the aggregate performance and focused on the importance of presenting the race gap, or the difference between white and African American performance.

Just as the second figure was needed to better understand the state's performance, similar information would be necessary for schools and school districts, the council members reasoned. Without information beyond overall averages, performance of states or districts with a larger African American population could be labeled as inadequate when compared to states or districts

Figure 4.2. Graph Depicting State
Performance Gaps, from 1994 NAEP Reading Exam Data

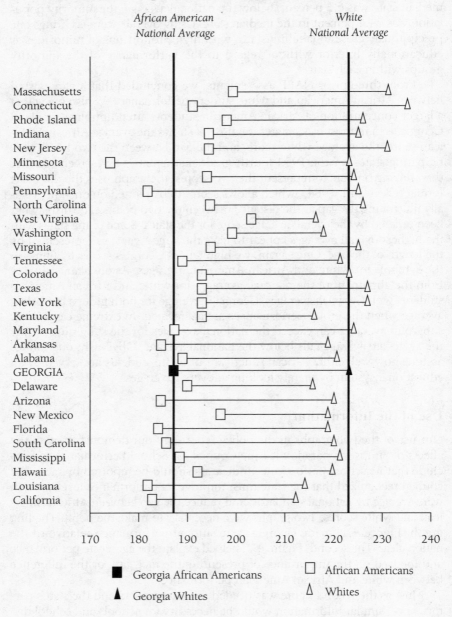

Note: Maine, North Dakota, Wisconsin, Iowa, New Hampshire, Montana, Connecticut, Wyoming, Nebraska, and Utah lacked a sufficient African American test-taking sample to compute a racial gap and thus were not included in this figure.

with a greater percentage of whites. Since their goal was to produce educational performance indicators and provide information that would lead to educational improvement for all groups in Georgia, disaggregating the data as shown in Figure 4.2 ensured that African American educational performance was not masked in overall scores and that the display of the data would not give inappropriate perceptions of performance.

Conclusion

Two questions inevitably arose: Which graph or interpretation is correct? Is Georgia below average, or almost exactly average? The answers are that both methods are correct and that how Georgia is ranked depends on the method used. National scorekeepers will keep ranking states on aggregate means, as in Figure 4.1. This method avoids controversy. Figure 4.2, which shows differences in performance by variables such as race and income, makes it clear that the educational system does not serve every student equally as well. Because this implication is so controversial and because finding solutions to the disparity is not easy, many will simply choose to avoid the issue.

In addition, methods such as those used in Figure 4.2 can be seen as self-serving. When this method results in an improved picture of performance, the media and the public perceive it as a defensive move (Henry, 1996). As in our example, Georgia's educational performance appeared better using our method than using the traditional method.

While the weighting method presented by Wainer (1986) as a means of adjusting or correcting aggregated data is useful, it appears to be a mathematical sleight of hand to skeptics and critics of public education. Weighting the data by racial proportions provides another way of looking at the information while overcoming the effects of Simpson's paradox, though it appears to be self-serving for Georgia. On the NAEP 1992 fourth-grade math assessment, Georgia moved from an unweighted rank of twenty-sixth to a weighted rank of twelfth (Henry and Glymph, 1995). This method shows the averages that would have occurred if the proportions of African Americans and whites were the same in each state, but it ends up communicating a limited amount of information.

The aftermath of the controversy sparked by Herrnstein and Murray's book *The Bell Curve* (1994) has produced some cogent and interesting arguments about race, education, and intelligence (Hilliard, 1995). Assuredly, disaggregating data by race remains extremely controversial. Thus it would be irresponsible to disregard the consequences of publishing school performance data disaggregated by race in a way that makes the gap so clear. The graphical presentation of the data in Figure 4.2 makes it readily apparent to citizens, policymakers, and educators that performance gaps exist. In our presentations, we emphasize the concept of school performance and the inequitable distribution of resources and services to African American and white students. We clearly state the council's goal of improving the education of all students by reducing these gaps. Moreover, without measuring the gaps by presenting that information, we cannot be sure we are making progress in the services delivered to both African American and white students. With averages that combine scores of all races, it is impossible to know whether educational improvements are raising the performance of all groups or if the averages are climbing due primarily to higher scores in one group alone.

Often, publication of scores disaggregated by race have been shunted to the back pages of three-inch thick reports because of a belief that reporting racial gaps will only stir up controversy. The Council for School Performance in Georgia took a different view, based on the information presented in these graphs: without information and monitoring, the gaps will continue, and until the inequities are brought to the attention of policymakers, educators, and the public overall, educational performance in Georgia will continue to lag behind the rest of the nation. These graphs have been used in presentations for education and business groups across the state, including the state board of education, the state chambers of commerce board, and the largest gatherings of professional educators in the state. While the graphs remain controversial, the council has been commended for presenting a balanced perspective and bringing the issue out of the shadows.

The council's performance reports were distributed amid much media attention in the winter of 1995–96, and for the first time race gaps in test scores, attendance, and graduation rates were published for all schools and school districts that enrolled sufficient numbers of students in both racial groups. One local magazine selected the best schools in the region using what they described as the "tough as nails" report by the Council for School Performance. A school district has applied for charter school status, which allows exemptions from some state regulations, by pledging to improve performance on all measures set forth by the Council for School Performance, including those disaggregated by race. Of course, much work remains to reduce performance gaps between African American and whites and to improve overall performance, but the reporting of this information seems to have provided impetus for the work to receive priority in Georgia.

References

Beckford, I. A., and Cooley, W. W. *The Racial Achievement Gap in Pennsylvania: Pennsylvania Educational Policy Studies Report #18*. Pittsburgh: University of Pittsburgh, Learning Research and Development Center, 1993.

Bertin, J. *Seminology of Graphics: Diagrams, Networks, Maps*. (W. J. Berg, trans.). Madison: University of Wisconsin Press, 1983. (Originally published 1967.)

Cleveland, W. S. "Graphical Methods for Data Presentations: Full Scale Breaks, Dot Charts, and Multibased Logging." *American Statistician*, 1984, *38* (4), 270–280.

Corcoran, T., and Goertz, M. "Instructional Capacity and High-Performance Standards." *Educational Researcher*, 1995, *24* (9), 27–31.

Henry, G. T. *Graphing Data: Techniques for Display and Analysis*. Thousand Oaks, Calif.: Sage, 1995.

Henry, G. T. "Community Accountability: A Theory of Information, Accountability, and School Improvement." *Phi Delta Kappan*, 1996, *78* (1), 85–90.

Henry, G. T., and Glymph, A. *Toward Accountability and Improvement: Reporting Performance Indicators by Race*. Atlanta: Applied Research Center, Georgia State University, 1995.

Henry, G. T., and others. *Council for School Performance: 1995 Annual Report*. Atlanta: Applied Research Center, Georgia State University, 1995.

Herrnstein, R. J., and Murray, C. *The Bell Curve: Intelligence and Class Structure in American Life*. New York: Free Press, 1994.

Hilliard, A. G., III. "Either a Paradigm Shift or No Mental Measurement." *Psych Discourse*, 1995, 26 (10), 6–20.

National Center for Education Statistics. *NAEP 1992 Mathematics Report Card for the Nation and the States*. Report no. 23-ST06. Washington, D.C.: National Assessment for Educational Progress, U.S. Department of Education, 1993.

National Center for Education Statistics. *1994 NAEP Reading: A First Look. Findings from the National Assessment of Educational Progress*. Washington: National Assessment for Education Progress, U.S. Department of Education, 1995.

Simpson, E. H. "The Interpretation of Interaction Contingency Tables." *Journal of the Royal Statistical Society*, 1951, *Series B* (13), 238–241.

Tufte, E. H. *The Visual Display of Quantitative Information*. Cheshire, Conn.: Graphics Press, 1983.

Wainer, H. "Minority Contributions to the SAT Score Turnaround: An Example of Simpson's Paradox." *Journal of Educational Statistics*, 1986, *11* (4), 239–244.

ALVIN GLYMPH *is research associate for the Applied Research Center of the School of Policy Studies at Georgia State University.*

GARY T. HENRY *is director of the Applied Research Center and associate professor in the Departments of Public Administration and Political Science in the School of Policy Studies at Georgia State University.*

Although double bar charts are commonly used to report a change
in quantity, they can obscure information and make analysis
difficult. Dot charts coupled with ordered category clustering
offer a better alternative.

Beyond Double Bar Charts: The Value of Dot Charts with Ordered Category Clustering for Reporting Change in Evaluation Research

James M. Sinacore

When conducting evaluations, researchers frequently examine change over time. An evaluation of a human services program would usually look at change among different parts or divisions of the agency that implements it. For example, consider a philanthropic organization that funds research in five areas of health care. The board of directors might want to examine the change in the number and amount of grants that were awarded over two funding cycles. In addition, they would probably want to compare that change among the five areas of health care.

Although change over time is important to evaluate, it poses a problem when quantities are displayed as a function of time, especially in a double bar graph. Variation of base values and the general magnitude of values can obscure information about change on a graph. And it becomes more difficult when there are more units.

As an example I present a double bar graph published in a university newspaper to show readers change in student enrollment over a decade. The original graph did a poor job of communicating the information. What follows is a description of the original graph and the information that was gleaned from it. I critique the graph and then offer alternative visual displays of the same information that incorporate techniques and principles described by experts in graphical analysis (see, for example, Chambers, Cleveland, Kleiner, and Tukey, 1983; Cleveland, 1985, 1993; Tufte, 1983).

NEW DIRECTIONS FOR EVALUATION, no. 73, Spring 1997 © Jossey-Bass Publishers

The Original Graph and Interpretation

In February 1994 the front page of *The Loyola Phoenix,* a newspaper of an urban Midwestern university, featured a story with the headline "Undergrad Enrollment Changes Widespread: Nursing Makes Gains, Business Losses" (DeCarlo, 1994). The accompanying graph showed the enrollment for students registered in thirty university departments and for students who were undeclared during the academic years of 1984 and 1992. Figure 5.1 is a careful replication of the graph as it appeared in the newspaper.

In the corresponding article, the author reported that the nursing department had the largest increase in enrollment over the decade. The education, psychology, and sociology departments also had large increases in enrollment. Enrollments in the fine arts and communication departments were on the rise.

The article concluded with a brief discussion of enrollment decreases. It mentioned chemistry as a department that had lost enrollment and noted that business was the major with the largest decrease in enrollment.

The visual display in Figure 5.1 was created with Microsoft Excel. It contains five features that complicate the analysis. First, the magnitude of the enrollments of undeclared students obscures the student enrollment data for

Figure 5.1. Double Bar Chart Showing Student Enrollment for Academic Years 1984 and 1992

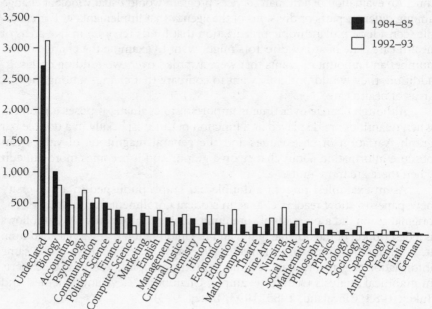

Source: DeCarlo, 1994.

the departments. In addition, the towering bars create a lot of unused space in the graph. In fact, 81 percent of the display area contains no information. Second, the department names are listed perpendicular to the horizontal axis, which makes it difficult to read them. Third, the grid lines are not needed. They are distracting and offer no help in decoding information, since most of the departments have enrollments with fewer than five hundred students. Fourth, the departments are ordered on the horizontal axis by enrollment in academic year 1984. Although this imposes some organization to the graph, it nevertheless makes it difficult to differentiate the departments that had an increase from those that had a decrease. This would be a natural concern for administrators and other stakeholders who want to analyze the change in enrollment over the decade.

Finally, the use of a double bar chart to describe change is, in and of itself, a problem. If the goal is to inform the reader about *change* in enrollment, why plot the actual enrollment figures? Double bar charts encumber the reader with more information than is needed to analyze change. This type of display forces readers to assess differences themselves, which could lead to perceptual errors. For example, the enrollment increase in the nursing department as seen in Figure 5.1 captures the readers' attention. In reality, the absolute difference in the enrollment for undeclared students is *slightly larger* than that for nursing students. This is explainable in terms of Weber's law, which states that the greater the magnitude of stimulation, the greater the change in stimulation that must occur before a difference can be perceived (Haber and Hershenson, 1980).

The Revised Visual Displays

Figures 5.2 and 5.3 present alternative displays of the student enrollment data. The overall goal for the revised displays was to effectively display the information so that readers could accurately interpret it. To that end, Cleveland's dot chart (1985) was chosen. Dot charts are graphs that have categories along the vertical axis and dots *over* the horizontal axis to denote some quantity, such as frequency. For reasons mentioned above, I decided to plot *change* in enrollment rather than the yearly enrollment figures. The actual change in enrollment (that is, the difference between 1984 and 1992) and the relative change (that is, the percentage increase or decrease) were plotted. Moreover, departments were clustered according to the type of change they experienced. Thus, departments with an increase were kept separate from those with a decrease. Within this major clustering, departments were then ordered according to the magnitude of enrollment change. The revised displays were constructed with SYSTAT for Windows 5.0.

The use of dots, as opposed to bars, in Figures 5.2 and 5.3 minimizes the redundancy of visual information, which according to Tufte (1983) is a desired feature. Bar charts inevitably possess redundancy, because bars are two-dimensional figures representing one-dimensional quantities. Consider, for example, the height of a bar that denotes a frequency. The heights of both the left-hand line and right-hand line of the bar convey the same information about the frequency. The top line of the bar only reiterates this information. Erasing any two lines of the bar does not subtract any information. Shading, cross-hatching, and adding numerical values create further redundancy. Dots, though two-dimensional figures, help to minimize redundancy by occupying small, fixed areas.

Insights. Figure 5.2 shows change in enrollment. The departments in each cluster are ordered from greatest to least amount of change. The top portion of the graph lists departments that experienced an increase in enrollment, ordered from greatest to least increase. The bottom portion of the graph shows the same for departments that experienced a decrease. The discontinuity of dots allows the reader to easily visualize the two main clusters of departments. The figure reveals more information than the original graph. For example, readers can clearly see that the change in enrollment is slightly higher for undeclared students than for nursing students. University administrators (or other types of program evaluators) would certainly want to know how enrollment information for undeclared students had changed over time. Technically speaking, then, it was the undeclared students who had the highest increase in enrollment frequency.

DeCarlo (1994) stated that the education department had a large increase in enrollment, which Figure 5.2 also illustrates. However, one can see that the English department had a similar increase. This fact is not easily seen in the double bar chart (Figure 5.1). Again, we see Weber's law in action.

The fine arts, communication, psychology, and sociology departments were reported to be among those on the increase. Figure 5.2 corroborates this but shows that the history, anthropology, and criminal justice departments had similar or greater increases than the sociology department. This fact is hidden in the double bar chart.

In terms of enrollment decreases, DeCarlo (1994) stated that business was the major that took the hardest hit. Most likely, the author added the losses for the accounting, finance, marketing, and management departments (or a combination thereof) and called it "business." As seen in the dot chart, the largest drop in enrollment was in the computer science department. Moreover, there were four departments that had a larger loss in enrollment than the chemistry department—although the latter was highlighted by DeCarlo (1994).

Relative Change. Figure 5.3 shows the dot chart for the relative, or percentage, change in enrollment over the decade. Departments are arranged on the ordinate, from greatest relative increase to greatest relative decrease. This creates a smooth display of dots across the entire graph. The two clusters (the departments that grew and those that shrunk) are separated by the reference line at the zero point. Dots to the right of the line represent departments with an enrollment increase. Dots to the left of the line represent those with an enrollment decrease. The design of Figure 5.3 is not as effective as Figure 5.2 for distinguishing clusters, but it can be a useful alternative in particular contexts.

In Figure 5.3, one can see that the nursing and education departments are among those with the greatest increases. The unexpected finding, however, is

Figure 5.2. A Dot Chart Showing
the Numerical Change in Student Enrollment

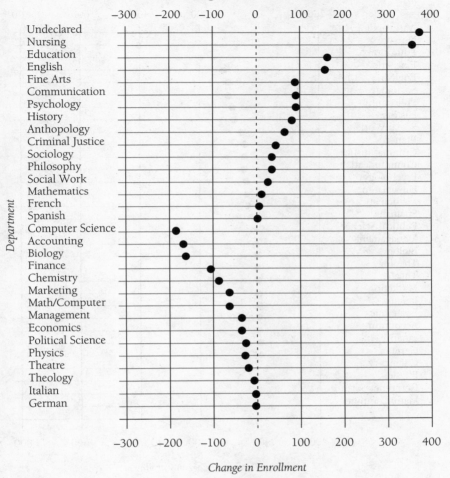

Change in Enrollment

that the enrollment in the anthropology department increased by 700 percent, from ten to eighty students! This is an important fact that is completely overlooked when analyzing raw change data. Although the enrollment of undeclared students showed the highest numerical increase, the anthropology department had the highest relative increase.

Conclusion

Double bar charts are inefficient for describing change, because they typically present information about two quantities rather than the change in those quan-

Figure 5.3. A Dot Chart Showing the Relative Change in Student Enrollment

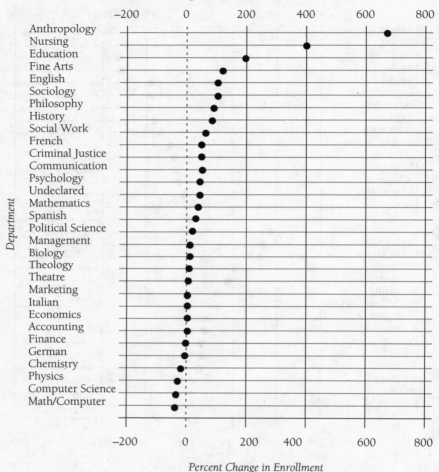

Percent Change in Enrollment

tities. The reader has to assess differences by visual inspection, which makes analyses vulnerable to perceptual error. Dot charts that report actual and relative change are better alternatives. Categories should be clustered according to like change (increase or decrease) and then ordered within those clusters by the magnitude of change.

References

Chambers, J. M., Cleveland, W. S., Kleiner, B., and Tukey, P. A. *Graphical Methods for Data Analysis.* Pacific Grove, Calif.: Brooks/Cole, 1983.

Cleveland, W. S. *The Elements of Graphing Data.* Belmont, Calif.: Wadsworth, 1985.

Cleveland, W. S. *Visualizing Data.* Summit, N.J.: Hobart, 1993.

DeCarlo, F. "Undergrad Enrollment Changes Widespread: Nursing Makes Gains, Business Loses." *The Loyola Phoenix,* February 2, 1994, pp. 1, 4.

Haber, R. N., and Hershenson, M. *The Psychology of Visual Perception.* (2nd ed.) Austin, Tex.: Holt, Rinehart and Winston, 1980.

Tufte, E. R. *The Visual Display of Quantitative Information.* Cheshire, Conn.: Graphics Press, 1983.

JAMES M. SINACORE is research director and assistant professor in the Department of Family Medicine at the University of Illinois at Chicago.

PART THREE

Displaying Trends

*Too often, the data format, rather than the objectives of the
presentation, drives graphic design. Control charts more effectively
illustrate processes over time than the more typically used bar
charts—even when additional graphics are required to fulfill
the objectives of the data presentation.*

Using Graphics to Convey Meaningful Comparison over Time

Robin S. Turpin

In the absence of national health care reform, third-party payers continue to
determine the length of hospital stays and other health care expenditures. Hospitals have struggled to assess the impact of this phenomenon on resource uti-
lization and patient outcomes. In an attempt to do so, we conducted a study
of stroke patients at a large physical medicine and rehabilitation hospital. We
included a bar graph in the report to illustrate changes in lengths of stay over
time for that facility's stroke patients, compared to changes nationwide.

The graph was widely disseminated among the hospital's clinical staff and
administrators, most of whom had little experience with interpreting data. The
graph's objectives were twofold: (1) to determine whether changes to enhance
quality and increase efficiency had impacted lengths of stay at the hospital and
(2) to identify whether lengths of stay for stroke patients in this hospital were
comparable to those reported nationally for patients in similar rehabilitative
settings. This information was needed to assess whether changes in lengths of
stay were influenced mostly by program improvements or by other pressures
that affected length of stay nationwide.

The greatest challenge was to present comparative data over time, given
that the national data were aggregated on a quarterly basis. Figure 6.1 is a
result of working within these constraints.

The Original Graph

Figure 6.1 is the original bar graph used to identify changes in lengths of stay
for stroke patients at the hospital and nationally. Hospital data were collected
through a computerized patient records system, downloaded into a program

evaluation database, and analyzed via the Statistical Package for the Social Sciences (SPSS). Data were graphed using Harvard Graphics and copied into a WordPerfect file to add report text. Means and confidence intervals reported by quarter for a twenty-seven month period were provided by the national database.

Figure 6.1 is easily read and understood. Readers can determine whether the hospital had lengths of stay greater or less than the national mean for any given quarter. They can also gain a general sense concerning the impact of interventions. For example, in April 1994, multidisciplinary team conferences were changed from biweekly to weekly. A mean drop of five days was experienced by the hospital during this quarter, without a corresponding drop in the national data. There was an additional drop the next quarter, with a fairly stable length of stay experienced over the next five quarters.

Figure 6.1. Bar Graph Comparing Hospital and National Data on Stroke Patient Lengths of Stay, by Quarter

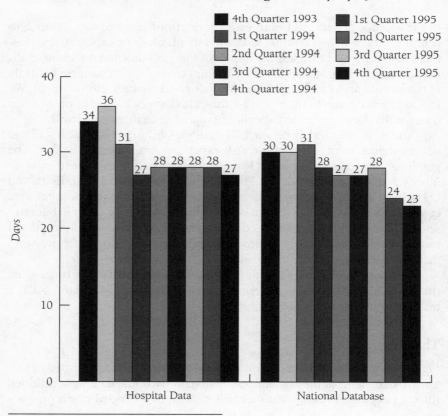

Hospital N = 726; National Database N = 122,400

Clearly Figure 6.1 provides important information, yet it also leaves several questions unanswered. Are the differences between the hospital's and the national lengths of stay significant? Should additional interventions be developed to further address efficiency of care and lower lengths of stay? Did the change to weekly team conferences have a significant impact? Should weekly team conferences be instituted for other programs (for example, for the spinal cord injury program)? Figure 6.1 leaves these questions largely unanswered.

Two Revised Graphs

Two revised graphics are recommended to fully illustrate changes in lengths of stay. The first objective of the original graphic was to determine whether programmatic changes to enhance quality and increase efficiency had impacted lengths of stay *over time*. Using SPSS, we created a control chart to plot the hospital's data over time and to demonstrate the variability associated with lengths of stay. (Other commonly available software packages, such as Excel, can produce these charts as well). Any time period can be chosen for study, so the analysis was not limited to quarterly data. In this case, monthly mean lengths of stay illustrated the dramatic impact of the intervention, while quarterly mean lengths of stay understated the impact.

The graph in Figure 6.2 plots lengths of stay on the vertical axis and monthly means on the horizontal axis. The centerline indicates the mean length of stay for the entire distribution. Key features of control charts are upper and lower control limits. These control limits are similar, theoretically, to confidence intervals and are calculated so that points falling outside their limits or in any other nonrandom pattern have a 5 percent probability of occurring by chance alone. Control limits are calculated at three standard deviations (generally referred to as 3-sigma) above and below the centerline. The simultaneous inference associated with the trend data necessitates a calculation of 3-sigma to achieve a 5 percent error rate. In clinical applications, control limits often exhibit "stair step" lines that reflect variable sample sizes.

Since every process exhibits some variation over time, control limits enable the user to detect whether any changes are significant. A process exhibits nonrandom, and therefore significant, variation if any of the following are true (Brassard, 1989):

- Any observation in the distribution falls outside the control limits.
- Two of three observations fall in the outer third of the area between the centerline and either control limit.
- Four of five observations fall in the outer two-thirds of the area between the centerline and either control limit.
- Nine or more consecutive observations fall on either side of the centerline.
- There is a run in the data, with six consecutive observations consistently decreasing or increasing.

Figure 6.2. X-Bar Chart for Stroke Patient Lengths of Stay

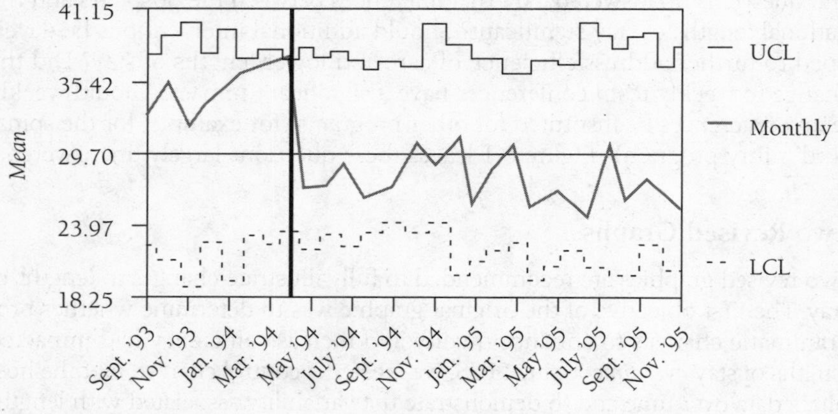

Note: Vertical line in April 1994 denotes introduction of weekly team conferences.
Distribution average = 29.70; N = 726; sigma level = 3.

- Fourteen consecutive observations alternate up and down.
- Fifteen consecutive observations cluster near the centerline.

The X-bar chart is one of the most common type of control charts, demonstrating means for a series of time periods, whether months, days, or hours. The X-bar chart in Figure 6.2 depicts nonrandom variation within a process. The data points in February, March, and April 1994 are grouped near the upper control limit, indicating that the *before* and *after* intervention lengths of stay are significantly different from each other.

Control charts were developed for quality improvement, where the objective is to observe changes in a given process over time. Clearly Figure 6.2 accomplishes more in this regard than Figure 6.1. The control chart provides a dramatic illustration of the effectiveness of the intervention, accompanied by an assessment of its statistical significance.

The second revised graph is a hi-lo chart created with Harvard Graphics. Figure 6.3 illustrates differences between length of stay for the hospital and other hospitals in the national database. This graph meets the second objective of the original graph, which was to identify whether the hospital's lengths of stay for stroke patients were comparable to lengths of stay reported nationally for patients in similar rehabilitative settings.

For the national comparison, data had to be presented by quarter, since this was the time frame provided. Figure 6.3 does not illustrate the means for the national data, but instead uses the 95 percent confidence intervals as provided by the national database. The thick gray bars represent these confidence intervals, while the thin black bars illustrate the quarterly mean for the hospital. There are two reasons for using confidence intervals instead of

Figure 6.3. Hi-Lo Graph Comparing Hospital Mean and National Database Expected Range for Stroke Patient Lengths of Stay

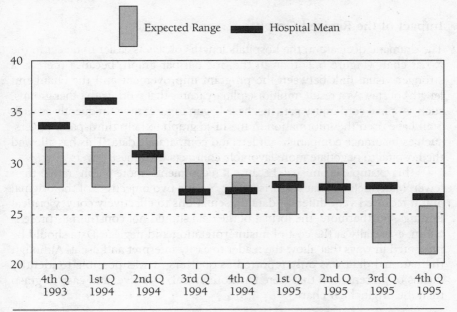

Note: Hospital means that fall outside the national range are significantly different from the expected. Hospital N = 726; national N = 122,400; bars represent the expected range, based on national data.

means. First, the probability that the length of stay for any individual hospital will match an exact norm consistently is quite low. Yet not matching the exact norm may erroneously lead users unfamiliar with data analysis to conclude that there is a problem with this length of stay in the hospital. By providing an expected range, confidence intervals enable a more reasonable interpretation of the data. Hospital means that fall within this range are still considered to reflect the national norms. Second, the hi-lo chart displays statistically significant differences between the two groups for each quarter, critical information that the original bar graph was unable to provide. Readers can easily determine whether the hospital data are different from the national, since hospital means that fall outside the national range are significantly different from the expected.

As illustrated in Figure 6.3, prior to the intervention in the third quarter, the hospital's lengths of stay were significantly longer than expected. The intervention of the weekly team conferences impacted lengths of stay, which remained stable and within the expected ranges over the next five months. In the last two quarters of 1995 there was a drop in the national lengths of stay, without a corresponding drop in the hospital's lengths of stay. While clearly the weekly team conferences had influenced the initial drop in lengths of stay, another intervention was needed if the hospital were to remain competitive with the national averages.

Impact of the Revised Graphs

The dramatic decrease in the hospital's lengths of stay is easier to detect in the X-bar chart (Figure 6.2) than in the original bar graph, because there is a stronger visual link between the program improvement and the change in lengths of stay. As a result, multidisciplinary teams that work with other groups, such as spinal cord injury patients, have begun to meet more frequently as well. Staff have used the information in the hi-lo graph to help third-party payers, such as insurance companies, understand comparative data. This has allowed the hospital to negotiate more favorable contracts with these payers.

This example is unusual, because it recommends more graphs rather than fewer. Many believe that fewer is better. Yet the two objectives of the original graph required very different data presentations to effectively convey critical findings. Furthermore, the format of the data should not constrain its presentation, especially at the cost of misinterpretation and neglect. Data should be presented in ways that allow the reader to easily interpret and use it. Although the national data was only reported as quarters, it was possible to identify means of presentation that were far more useful, intuitive, and easy to grasp than the original bar chart.

References

Brassard, M. *The Memory Jogger Plus: Featuring Seven Management and Planning Tools.* Methuen, Mass.: Quality Press, 1989.

Additional Resources

Berwick, D. M., Godfrey, A. B., and Roessner, J. *Curing Health Care: New Strategies for Quality Improvement.* San Francisco: Jossey-Bass, 1990.

Finison, L. J., Finison, K. S., and Bliersbach, C. M. "The Use of Control Charts to Improve Health Care Quality." *Journal of Healthcare Quality*, 1993, 15 (1), 9–23.

Gitlow, H., Gitlow, H., Oppenheim, A., and Oppenheim, R. *Tools and Methods for the Improvement of Quality.* Homewood, Ill.: Irwin, 1989.

McLaughlin, C. P., and Kaluzny, A. D. *Continuous Quality Improvement in Health Care.* Gaithersburg, Md.: Aspen, 1994.

ROBIN S. TURPIN is director of outcome information at the Rehabilitation Institute of Chicago and assistant professor in the Department of Physical Medicine and Rehabilitation at Northwestern University Medical School.

Solutions to two common time series graphing problems are presented.
The revised graph in the first group shows the difference between
a criterion level and an actual level of financial performance;
the second shows the behavior of statewide student cohorts.

Time Series Graphs on Financial Performance and Cohort Dropout Rates

Kathleen Sullivan

The graphs presented in this chapter are from recent reports to the Mississippi legislature. They illustrate solutions to problems that are common when reporting information on a time series. One problem entails showing a difference between two time-related trends over the same period. Column and line graphs are used to show the difference between a criterion condition (in this case, payments that a small, rural utility must make to meet its financial obligations) and an actual or projected condition (amounts the district is likely to be able to pay). This example is comparable to illustrating a projection of a budget deficit or the gap between services needed and services provided.

Another problem in presenting time series data entails showing effects of a program that is phased in (that is, affects different groups at different times). Education programs are sometimes introduced this way. Phased implementation can result in a distinctly different program experience for each student cohort. In this chapter a line graph shows differences in program effects for a series of cohorts. This approach offers an alternative to graphing averages that include data for participants and nonparticipants, which can mask program effects.

Evaluation Audiences

Mississippi's Joint Legislative Committee on Performance Evaluation and Expenditure Review (PEER), created by statute in 1973, provides evaluative

Author's note: David J. Pray, Barbara Y. Hamilton, Stephen R. Miller, H. L. Whiting, Mitchell H. Adcock, Max K. Arinder, and Ava L. Welborn helped develop the graphs and evaluation reports that are the subject of this chapter.

information to the state legislature. The committee is made up of ten legislators—five representatives and five senators. It employs a staff of approximately twenty-six analysts, managers, and support staff to conduct evaluations and prepare evaluation reports.

The staff reports evaluation findings primarily to the Mississippi legislature, although the audience for PEER's evaluation reports includes many stakeholders outside the legislature. The other stakeholders include administrators and staff in the programs that are evaluated, the general public, and the media. Carefully designed graphs provide the desired clarity, directness, and brevity to communicate effectively with all of these audiences.

Graphs used in two PEER reports are discussed below. The first report focused on a small natural gas district and included the graphs in Figures 7.1, 7.2, and 7.3. The second report, which included the graphs in Figures 7.4 and 7.5, examined the impact of a provision of the state's public school attendance law. Although the reports containing these graphs describe evaluation results for two very different programs, performance over time is a common theme in all of the graphs.

Illustrating a Gap Between a Criterion Condition and Actual Performance

The first three graphs compare a conventional presentation of time series data obtained from financial reports (Figures 7.1 and 7.2) with another approach that helps policymakers anticipate long-term viability (Figure 7.3). In this case, evaluators supplemented historical information shown in two column graphs (Figures 7.1 and 7.2) with financial projections shown in a line graph (Figure 7.3).

Other uses for this kind of column and line graph are to illustrate gaps between related financial trends, differences between services that are needed and those provided, or variations in performance at two or more sites (such as schools, hospitals, job training sites, regional mental health centers) over time. This approach can also effectively illustrate time-related variations in the difference between average performance of the highest and lowest quartiles on a variable of interest (for example, worker productivity or academic achievement).

Problem Statement. In response to a legislative request, PEER examined the financial viability of a rural natural gas district, a political subdivision created by the legislature to purchase and deliver natural gas to customers in northeastern Mississippi (Mississippi Joint Legislative Committee on Performance Evaluation and Expenditure Review, 1996). The legislature authorized the natural gas district to pay for construction of an underground gas transmission and delivery system by issuing revenue bonds, a category of bonds that are repaid through a specified stream of revenue, such as collections from gas sales.

Purpose of the Evaluation. About eight years after the natural gas district issued $2.78 million in revenue bonds and began building the delivery system, a legislator from that area reported that the district was experiencing severe financial problems. In a legislative session subsequent to the original

Figure 7.1. Column Graph of Revenue Versus Expenses

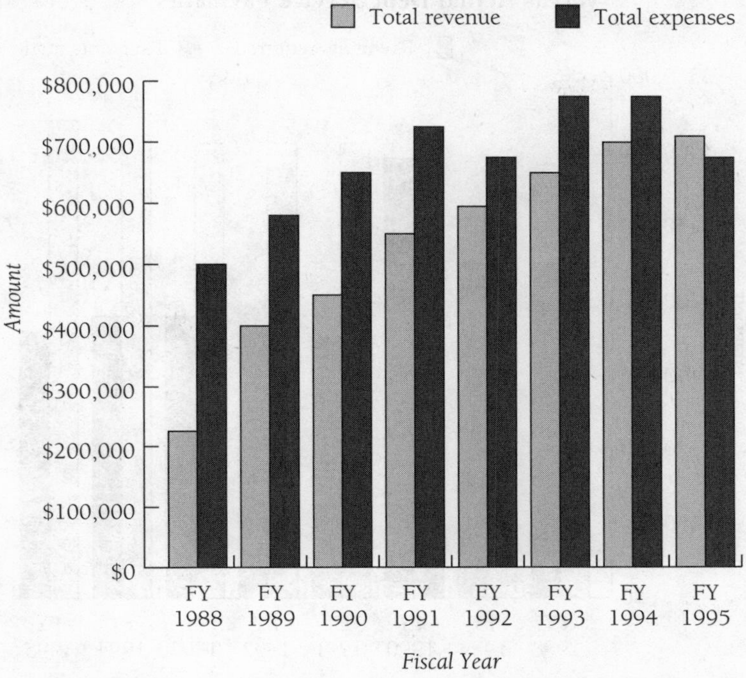
Total revenue
Total expenses
$800,000
$700,000
$600,000
$500,000
$400,000
$300,000
$200,000
$100,000
$0
Amount
FY 1988
FY 1989
FY 1990
FY 1991
FY 1992
FY 1993
FY 1994
FY 1995
Fiscal Year

bond issue, the district had asked the legislature for additional bonding authority. The legislature had refused the district's request, but legislators knew they might be asked again to act on behalf of the district. Was the utility financially sound? For example, were its revenues adequate to support necessary expenditures? Also, if the utility were to default on its bonds, would the state be responsible for its debt? To find answers to these questions, PEER evaluated the district's financial condition and researched the state's responsibility for the district's debt should the district default on its bond obligations.

Purpose of the Financial Projection Graph. PEER found that the natural gas district's annual financial obligations had exceeded its revenues from the time it had become fully operational eight years earlier. By 1995, when PEER conducted its review, the district had defaulted on $360,000 in bond principal and owed a considerable amount in past-due interest. In addition to pressing past-due obligations, the district annually faced a daunting schedule of current principal and interest obligations.

District directors and staff, who had not thoroughly analyzed the district's financial condition, were hopeful that a slight upward trend they detected in revenues would help the district avoid financial ruin. To assess the validity of the district's optimism, PEER analysts determined the principal and interest amounts that would come due each year, anticipated payment of past-due

Figure 7.2. Column Graph of Required Versus Actual Debt Service Payments

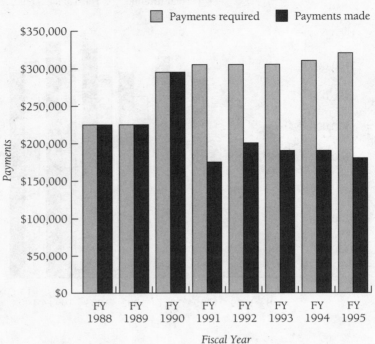

principal and interest, and projected annual operating expenses (somewhat conservatively) and likely revenues (rather generously). PEER concluded that the district was too deeply in debt to hold out much hope of recovery by 2009, the year when all bonds were originally to have been retired. As the district's debt payments continued to fall short of combined past-due and current obligations, interest on the past-due principal and interest would continue to mount, decreasing the likelihood of recovery.

PEER staff decided the report detailing PEER's findings should include a graph conveying the debilitating cumulative effect of years of low revenue and missed principal payments. The graph would have to present results of a complex analysis in a way that would clearly and frankly illustrate the district's long-term financial outlook.

Original Graphs. The initial graphs showed historical data—the difference between revenue and expenses over the district's eight-year existence (Figure 7.1) and the difference between required and actual debt service payments over the same eight-year period (Figure 7.2). This information is usually found in a company's income statement. Data on required and actual debt service payments typically would be found in other financial statements. The graphs

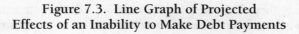

Figure 7.3. Line Graph of Projected Effects of an Inability to Make Debt Payments

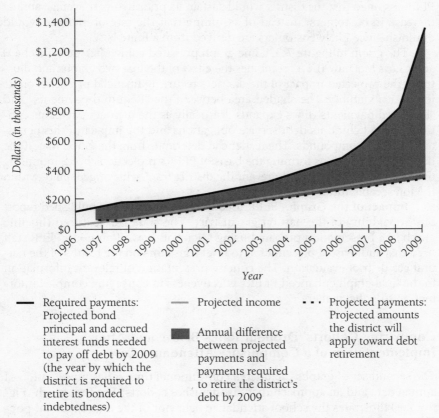

in Figures 7.1 and 7.2, prepared using Microsoft Excel 4.0, are column graphs featuring two columns per fiscal year. Each shows a difference in two related trends affecting the district's financial status. PEER included these graphs in its report because they provide important background information. However, neither of the original graphs effectively conveyed the impact that the district's mounting cumulative debt likely would exert on its financial future. Although legislators might consider historical information interesting, future viability was the issue of greatest concern.

Revised Graph. After further analyzing historical data and projecting likely revenues (primarily from gas sales), expenses (including salary, professional services, operating, interest, and income expenses), and bond principal payments due, analysts prepared the graph in Figure 7.3.

PEER used accepted practice in projecting revenues and expenditures, though it leaned slightly toward optimism when projecting the district's revenues.

This approach, they reasoned, would avoid both undue optimism and unnecessary alarm among stakeholders. For example, in projecting district revenues, PEER assumed that the district would sustain its prior five-year average annual increase in customers, instead of assuming that the rate of increase would diminish since likely customers are derived from a finite base.

The graph in Figure 7.3, a line graph prepared using Microsoft Excel 4.0 and Claris McDraw II 1.1, combines the effect of the first two graphs and illustrates the projected impact of the district's recurring financial problems on its long-term viability. The shaded area between the "Required payments" and "Projected payments" lines expands drastically as the district's payments continue to lag behind its debt service obligations and the impact of this persistent shortfall compounds. The reader can determine from the graph that, if the financial assumptions forming the basis of PEER's projections hold, mounting debt service obligations will prevent the district from achieving viability within the foreseeable future.

Impact of the Graph. PEER used the third graph in its published report on the viability of the natural gas district. The staff also featured this line graph in a presentation prepared using Microsoft PowerPoint 4.0. PEER staff used this audiovisual presentation to brief legislators on the results of the natural gas district evaluation. The concise presentation of relevant information in the final graph enhanced PEER's effectiveness in conveying complex information to policymakers.

Comparing Cohorts' Dropout Rates Before and After Implementation of a Compulsory Attendance Law

The second set of graphs included a conventional time series presentation of annual data and an approach that distinguishes cohorts. The first graph (Figure 7.4) illustrates the school attendance behavior of the entire student population. The second graph (Figure 7.5) compares various cohorts subject to a compulsory attendance law to a cohort that was not legally compelled to attend school.

Problem Statement. In 1977 the Mississippi legislature enacted a law phasing in compulsory attendance by requiring that seven-year-olds be compelled to attend school in 1977–78. The law added a year to that maximum age each successive school year until the 1983–84 school term, at which point the maximum compulsory attendance age would be thirteen. The legislature later amended the law to require attendance from six years of age through age seventeen. The 1977 law also established "school attendance counselor" positions across the state; subsequent amendments expanded the program, placed it under the state's youth court system, and changed the title of attendance counselors to "school attendance officers." Although the later law increased the number of officers in an attempt to improve program effectiveness, qualifications and enforcement authority of attendance officers were minimal during the program's first decade. In 1987 the legislature enacted a requirement that

Figure 7.4. Conventional Time Series Graph of Annual Data

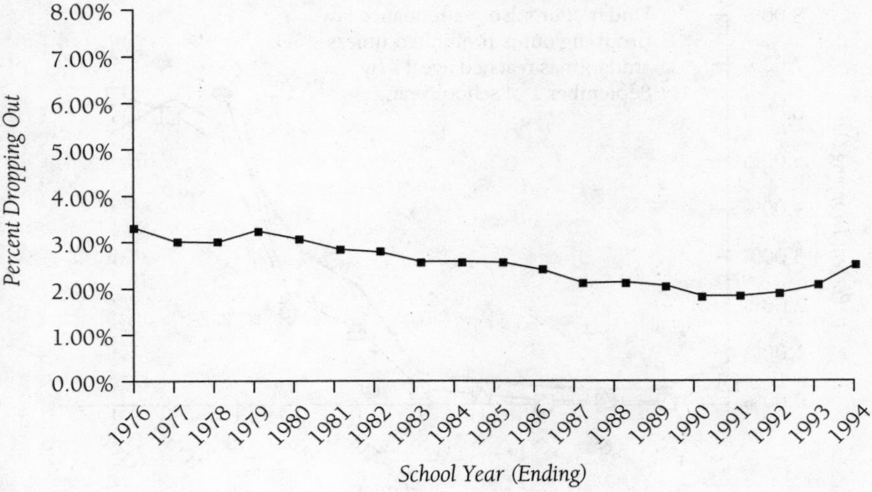

Percent Dropping Out (y-axis)

School Year (Ending) (x-axis)

attendance officers hold college degrees, and in 1992 it granted attendance officers limited enforcement authority.

Purpose of the Evaluation. Legislators' need for information on the operation and effectiveness of a school attendance officer program prompted PEER's review (Mississippi Joint Legislative Committee on Performance Evaluation and Expenditure Review, 1994). Just prior to the study, the legislature had enacted a bill requiring PEER to determine the most appropriate organizational location for the program. The PEER committee directed its staff to assess the program's effectiveness and determine where the program should be located.

Purpose of the Cohort Dropout Rate Graph. An experimental or quasi-experimental design would have permitted PEER to definitively assess the effectiveness of the program. Since this type of research design would require conditions that the program could not satisfy, PEER could only present data on school attendance and dropout rates prior to and following implementation of the law that mandated attendance and established the attendance officer program.

Given the conditions of the evaluation, the evaluators could not hope to distinguish between (1) the effect that simply compelling attendance might have exerted on dropout rates and (2) the effectiveness of school attendance officers, who were charged with preventing students from skipping school and dropping out. Also impossible was discerning between the effects of these two components of the compulsory attendance law (mandatory attendance and implementation of the attendance officer program) and the influence of any intervening variables, such as curricular and societal changes. PEER chose to present time series data on dropout rates, deriving policy implications from the trend analysis while avoiding unsupported conclusions of causality.

Figure 7.5. Graph That Distinguishes Cohorts

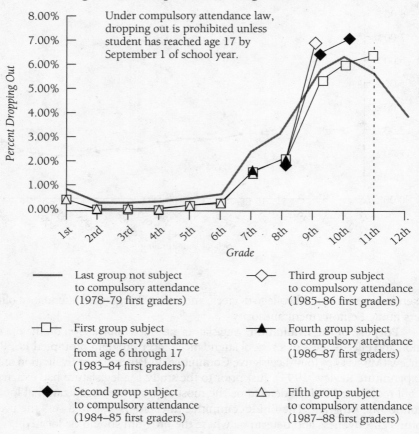

Even basic trend data were sufficient to demonstrate that the effect of the compulsory attendance law was not strong enough to shift prevailing absentee rates or to prevent ever-increasing dropout rates among cohorts subject to the attendance law. Through a graphic presentation of comparative data, PEER staff sought to inform legislators of recent and somewhat alarming dropout rates among early teens subject to compulsory attendance laws.

Original Graph. A standard time-series presentation (Figure 7.4), prepared using Microsoft Excel 4.0, shows annual statewide dropout rates spanning the period from just prior to the implementation of the compulsory attendance and school attendance officer law through the 1993–94 school year. However, the information provided by this approach is of little value in examining dropout trends in relation to the compulsory attendance law, because statewide annual dropout rates inappropriately combine in a single data point the dropout rates for cohorts that were among the groups subject to compulsory attendance with data for cohorts that were not subject to the law. For example, the data point for the 1983–84 academic year in Figure 7.4 combines data for first- through eighth-graders, whose enrollment and attendance were subject to provisions of the compulsory attendance law, with data for ninth- through twelfth-graders, whose enrollment and attendance were not compelled by law (and therefore were not monitored by attendance officers).

Preparing a separate graph or a separate line for each grade would have permitted labeling to indicate whether a group was subject to the compulsory attendance law, but neither approach would have provided a practical solution. Twelve separate graphs would have been unwieldy, and showing annual dropout rates by grade on separate lines of the same graph would have necessitated insertion of a confusing series of break points, as successive grades fell under the compulsory attendance law.

Revised Graph. To provide discrete information on students who were subject to the compulsory attendance law, PEER analyzed and graphed dropout data by cohort (Figure 7.5). This graph was prepared using Microsoft Excel 4.0 and Claris McDraw II 1.1. Each cohort line in the graph represents a group of students that began school together as six-year-olds and worked their way through the system.

Only data on homogeneous cohorts (those subject to compulsory attendance throughout their school careers or not subject to this law at any time) are included in the graph. For example, the cohort represented by the heavy, shaded line is the last group to move through the grades that was not subject to the laws. That group entered first grade in 1978 and twelfth grade in 1989. Five years after that cohort entered first grade, the first cohort subject to the compulsory school attendance law throughout their school careers entered the system. That group, designated on the graph with open square data points, began school in 1983.

In addition to providing information on discrete groups of service recipients and nonrecipients, the cohort approach permitted presentation of data by grade level, facilitating identification of grades with a particularly high incidence of dropping out.

The reader can determine from the second graph that, regardless of the precise impact of the compulsory attendance law, any positive effect that the law might have exerted was not strong enough to prevent an increase in dropout rates in the higher grades among cohorts subject to the law, especially in grades 9 through 11. A slight but consistent difference between the baseline cohort (1978–79 first-graders) and later cohorts in grades 1 through 6, combined with a more substantial decline in dropout rates for seventh- and eighth-graders, may be evidence that passage of the law was associated with delays in dropping out. However, for the higher grades, the graph shows an increase in the difference between dropout rates of cohorts subject to compulsory attendance and the rates of the baseline cohort. This worsening of dropout rates in the higher grades may show that societal changes or other variables affecting later cohorts' enrollment rates in the early teen years apparently were so strong that they masked any effect that the compulsory attendance law might have exerted on enrollment rates among the groups.

Impact of the Graph. PEER published the cohort graph in a report that also described serious problems in attendance officer program operations. The PEER staff presented the cohort dropout graph, like the utility district line graph, in a PowerPoint briefing to legislators. The graph contributed to a body of evidence that prompted legislators to discuss the need for a more effective approach to preventing absenteeism and dropping out among Mississippi schoolchildren.

References

Mississippi Joint Legislative Committee on Performance Evaluation and Expenditure Review. *The Mississippi School Attendance Officers Program: A Joint Study by the PEER Committee and the John C. Stennis Institute of Government.* Jackson: Mississippi Joint Legislative Committee on Performance Evaluation and Expenditure Review, 1994.

Mississippi Joint Legislative Committee on Performance Evaluation and Expenditure Review. *A Review of the Viability of the Mantachie Natural Gas District and the State's Relationship to the District.* Jackson: Mississippi Joint Legislative Committee on Performance Evaluation and Expenditure Review, 1996.

KATHLEEN SULLIVAN *is evaluation division manager for the Mississippi Joint Legislative Committee on Performance Evaluation and Expenditure Review.*

This chapter draws attention to various evaluation concerns and their impact on the presentation of data. It emphasizes the importance of several graphics principles, including avoiding clutter, limiting the number of features in a graph, understanding the evaluation question, and knowing the audience.

Evaluation Concerns and the Presentation of Data

Mika'il DeVeaux

The primary function of program evaluation is to provide feedback to program managers, funders, and policymakers on whether desired goals are being achieved (Sullivan, 1992). Evaluation provides information on program design and planning (the program model), program monitoring (processes), outcomes, and economic efficiency (cost-benefit analyses and cost-effectiveness analyses) (Sullivan, 1992; Smith, 1991). The objective of evaluation research is usually to provide information requested by program funders and program managers, whereas the objective of basic research is to test a hypothesis (Smith, 1991). Since the objective of evaluation research differs from basic research, it makes sense that the presentation of the data would also differ.

The graphs in this chapter are from an evaluation report prepared for Domvol. (Domvol is a pseudonym for a not-for-profit organization located in the New York City area.) Domvol offers crisis housing ("Type A" housing in the graphs) and transitional housing ("Type B" housing), counseling, and other services for families that have survived abuse. Program evaluators were asked to determine how long clients were housed at Domvol and to compare the amount of time spent in crisis housing and transitional housing. Given this evaluation concern, evaluators had to determine how to best present the collected data in one graph.

The Data: From Collection to Presentation

The data were gathered by surveying counseling staff when clients were discharged from crisis or transitional housing. The analyst had to produce a single graph that answered many questions: How many clients have been

NEW DIRECTIONS FOR EVALUATION, no. 73, Spring 1997 © Jossey-Bass Publishers

discharged during the current reporting period? How long were discharged clients housed at Domvol? How many were housed at each site? To what extent do discharge rates vary by site?

A univariate analysis (a separate examination of individual variables) provides an exploratory look at the amount of time clients were housed at Domvol (Smith, 1991; Philliber, Schwab, and Sloss, 1980). Using the 6.0 version of the Statistical Package for the Social Sciences (SPSS), this was easily computed by subtracting the date clients entered Domvol from the date they were discharged. In this instance, the results yielded a cumbersome frequency distribution. Consequently, the data were grouped into various categories and the frequencies converted to percentages to obtain comparable measures of clients discharged from Domvol and its sites.

Selecting a Graph

The graphs were produced with Harvard Graphics for Windows. After grouping the data into fourteen categories, the analyst selected a line graph to display the results (Figure 8.1). The graph seemed cluttered, confusing, and visually misleading. Graphs with too many categories often look "scientific" and intimidating. Graphics gurus suggest that limiting the number of features in presentation graphs creates a better graph. The crisscrossing lines in the graph in Figure 8.1 give the impression that there are more than the actual three lines. Unintendedly, the rise and fall of the lines seem to suggest change over time. In addition, readers were unable to clearly distinguish the value labels associated with series markers.

Line graphs used for analytical purposes generally "depict relationships between categorically or continuously distributed data for two or more variables" and suggest direction or trends over time (Smith, 1991, p. 643). We found sophisticated use of line graphs in depictions of multiple observations over time, which are frequently found in time series or interrupted time series analyses (Cook and Campbell, 1979). Our intent was neither to suggest change over time nor to show direction. Instead, we wanted readers to be visually clear about the dispersion of the data, rather than to search for text explaining our intentions. While those familiar with line graphs may easily spot series and highlighted information, we needed a graph that an inexperienced reader could also decipher.

The Evaluation Question Provides Focus. Improving on the initial graph, we replaced it with one that was less visually demanding and displayed the answers to questions raised by Domvol staff. The number of features in the new and improved graph was limited by collapsing the categories. This helped to distinguish the main idea of the graph. One researcher suggested a cumulative line graph showing the percent remaining at select points in time (Figure 8.2). This would show the "flow" of the data, but that was not what we sought to communicate. Another researcher suggested inverting the data. This would enable readers to see the different rates at which clients left the

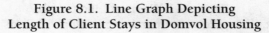

**Figure 8.1. Line Graph Depicting
Length of Client Stays in Domvol Housing**

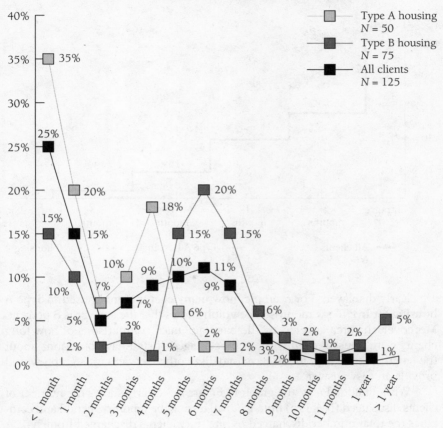

housing. Following the lines, Domvol staff would need only to identify the time period from which they wanted to take a reading. The legend details the actual number of clients and distinguishes the lines related to each site. In addition, the most important line has been thickened and its "line fit" made into a step. The "all clients" line is singled out to draw attention to the overall performance of Domvol. Furthermore, we changed the title of the graph from "Length of Client Stay in Domvol Housing" to "Percent Remaining in Domvol Housing." Doing so, however, suggested answers to questions different from those initially posed. Nevertheless, an accurate reading of the graph is possible by first reading the title, legend, x-axis, and finally the percentages. Compared to Figure 8.1, Figure 8.2 is much cleaner and easier to understand.

Even though the graph in Figure 8.2 was better than the one in Figure 8.1, it did not fit all our needs. We created the bar graph (Figure 8.3) to more effectively communicate the data. Answers to questions asked by Domvol staff

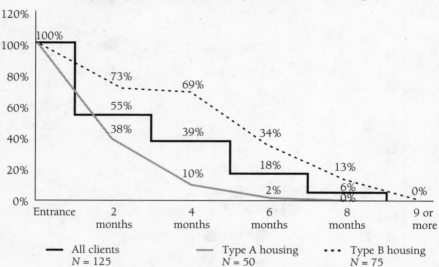

Figure 8.2. Revised Line Graph,
Depicting Percent Remaining in Domvol Housing

are clearly displayed. For example, how many clients were housed in Type A housing for five to six months? The graph shows that the answer is 8 percent. Moreover, the area covered by the bars facilitates comparisons of how long clients were housed, even without percentages. If staff have questions about the length of time they might have to deliver other services, this graph would provide an easy answer.

Without added text, the graph in Figure 8.3 clearly shows the number of clients discharged (N = 125) from Domvol during the reporting period and compares the total number discharged by site (fifty clients discharged from Type A housing and seventy-five clients discharged from Type B housing). It also shows how long various percentages of the discharged clients were housed and how this varied by site. Although the same data is used, the graph in Figure 8.2 does not communicate this information. Figure 8.2 may give the reader the impression that clients discharged during this reporting period entered Domvol housing at the same time. In fact, we had measured how long those clients who were discharged during a specified period of time had been housed at the different sites. Figure 8.2 answers the question, "How long do clients remain in Domvol housing?"

Program evaluators should not expect program staff and funders to be as "sophisticated" with research as they are. For some, the choice between Figures 8.2 and 8.3 may be one of preference. However, decisions about which graph to use should be focused by the objectives of the research and the audience for which the research is intended.

Evaluation Concerns Shape the Graph. There is no single best way to make a visual presentation. Hence, another factor that influences the choice of

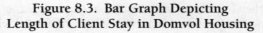

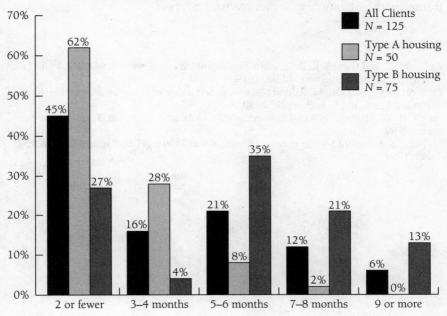

**Figure 8.3. Bar Graph Depicting
Length of Client Stay in Domvol Housing**

graph to use in a presentation is the extent to which the graph might appeal to a given audience. Evaluators need to know their audience. We settled on the bar graph in Figure 8.3 because the audience would consist mainly of laypeople, or those who were not researchers by profession. Even when this is not true, an analyst should never assume that the audience has specific knowledge about statistics or graphics. Even the simplest of graphs may be misread.

Conclusion

Evaluation concerns affect the presentation of data. When reducing data to graphs, evaluators should strive to avoid clutter and the temptation to squeeze too much information into a limited space. Limiting the number of features in a graph helps eliminate clutter and allows the reader to get to the main idea faster. It is also important to know what is being asked of the data and to be clear about the answers. Knowing who the audience is is equally important. What might be suitable for one group may not work with another. When making a graph, assume nothing about the background of the audience. The audience may not have a statistical or graphics background. Finally, before settling on a graph, several ideas should be tried. With today's graphics programs, ideas are as accessible as the click of a mouse. Graphics gurus all have principles and

74   CREATING EFFECTIVE GRAPHS

rules of thumb they follow to make the task of graphing easier. None of those principles are engraved in stone, but they may prove helpful when one is confronted with graphing data for an evaluation report.

References

Cook, T. D., and Campbell, D. T. *Quasi-Experimentation: Design and Analysis Issues for Field Settings.* Boston: Houghton Mifflin, 1979.

Philliber, S. G., Schwab, M. R., and Sloss, G. S. *Social Research: Guides to a Decision-Making Process.* Itasca, Ill.: F. E. Peacock, 1980.

Smith, H. W. *Strategies of Social Research.* (3rd ed.) Austin, Tex.: Holt, Rinehart and Winston, 1991.

Sullivan, T. J. *Applied Sociology: Research and Critical Thinking.* Old Tappan, N.J.: Macmillan, 1992.

MIKA'IL DEVEAUX is a data analyst with Philliber Research Associates, based in Accord, New York.

PART FOUR

Displaying Relationships

*A two-by-two table effectively presents the relationship between
a predictor and an outcome. Using fewer cells in the table focuses
the reader's attention on the contingent relationship.*

Some Visual Displays of Two-by-Two Data: Predicting Later Violent Behavior

James H. Derzon

Whether identifying risk factors for assigning individuals to treatment or examining the relationship between treatment and outcomes, evaluators often assess the patterns in moving from a particular status at one point in time to another status at a later point in time. However, laboratory experiments have shown that individuals tend to commit various errors in judgment when asked to make decisions based on this sort of conditional information (Dawes, 1988; Hogarth, 1987; Kahneman, Slovic, and Tversky, 1982). Since conditional information is difficult to present succinctly, researchers have traditionally used summative indices to present their findings. The zero-order correlation is one such statistical tool for indexing these regularities, but correlations do not tell the entire story and may even be misleading. Using the example of predicting an individual's violent behavior from knowledge of his or her prior condition, I will present some graphical techniques for making that information accessible to research audiences.

Since the magnitude of a correlation can vary independently from the natural base rate of the predictor (its natural rate of occurrence in a population), a strong correlation may tell relatively little about how well a risk factor would predict violent behavior and therefore would not be useful in determining cases for intervention. Given identical correlations with an outcome, risk factors may be associated with high rates of error in prediction, with the rate of false-positive identifications increasing as the base rate increases and the rate of false-negative identifications increasing as the base rate decreases (Derzon, 1996, p. 212). ("False positive" refers to the ratio of those positively identified by a predictor who do not display an outcome. Similarly, "false negative" refers to the ratio of those not identified by a predictor who do display the outcome.)

Using risk factors to target interventions requires weighing the costs associated with these different errors. For example, we would not want to direct clients into intervention using risk factors associated with high false-positive ratings when the intervention is expensive, stigmatizing, or highly intrusive. On the other hand, a high false-negative risk factor may have devastating effects when failure to provide treatment increases the consequences of the outcome. Because correlations do not provide information on the rate of these errors, it is often useful to dichotomize the data at some conventional, meaningful, or empirical level and consider these contingent relationships when assessing risk factors.

Therefore, examining the independent and conditional relationships between naturally occurring or imposed dichotomous predictive variables and the likelihood of a later outcome is necessary for identifying useful risk factors for intervention. In this example, we need to determine how useful a risk factor is as a determinant of future violent behavior. What is at issue here is the utility of assessing the independent probabilities of exhibiting an outcome given one's antecedent status on one or more dichotomized predictor variables. As a matter of practice, the antecedent conditions that justify intervention may often be viewed dichotomously. Above some threshold, an individual is considered to be at risk for an outcome and either qualifies or does not qualify for intervention. Because dichotomized data provides additional information about a relationship, it is both useful and appropriate in risk assessments. When the underlying data are continuous, both this information and product moment correlations need to be provided, since dichotomizing continuous data attenuates estimates of the strength of a relationship (McNemar, 1966, pp. 192–193).

It is difficult, however, to present contingent relationships without (1) directing attention to some subset of the data (for example, enumerating the *true-positives*), (2) presenting the *phi coefficient* and ignoring the independent contingencies altogether, or (3) overwhelming the reader by presenting either a series of two-by-two tables or one large table listing all cell values. One way to not overwhelm the reader and still present this complex and interrelated data is by presenting the data graphically. Using meta-analytic data collected to examine the efficacy of various antecedents for predicting later violent behavior, we turn attention now to contrasting some traditional and visual displays of conditional information.[1]

Presenting the Results from a Single Predictor

A first question when assessing the effectiveness of risk factors for selecting individuals for intervention is, "Are those who are above some threshold on a predictor more likely than those below the threshold to engage in later violent behavior?" To answer this question, researchers often present their data in a two-by-two contingency table, such as Table 9.1. This table contains the cell names and synthesized cell values for the average relationship of all predictors with later violent behavior. The values in this two-by-two table provide all the data necessary to assess the relationships among the dichotomized conditions of antecedent and outcome. When assessing the likelihood that those considered to be at risk according to some predictor will exhibit later violence, our attention is directed toward the value of cell A relative to the value of cells B and C. When the value in cell A is large relative to these other cells, we could conclude that being at risk disposes one to the outcome.

I want to emphasize that one should evaluate a risk factor by the relative and not absolute value of cell A. An increase in the value of cell B relative to cell A may indicate either that the predictor is sensitive to the suppressing effects of other conditions or that the suspected cause requires multiple facilitating conditions to achieve the outcome. Conversely, as the value of cell C relative to cell A increases, the number of other conditions that may give rise to the outcome's occurrence may also increase. Einhorn and Hogarth (1986) noted the contributions cells B and C make to causal inferencing, as these cells focus attention on either the multiplicity of causation (a backward inference based on cell C) or on the conditionality of causation (a forward inference based on cell B). Finally, cell D contains the reference population, which is essential for making estimates of incidence or prevalence. The units that are included in cell D completes the description of the populations to whom the results are generalizable. Thus, all four cells and their relations are necessary and sufficient for characterizing the relationship between two dichotomous variables.

The table can be contrasted with a graph of the same data, shown in Figure 9.1. In this figure, the grand mean predictor and outcome base rates can be observed, respectively, in the extreme left- and right-hand sides of the

Table 9.1. Two-by-Two Contingency Table Demonstrating the Relationship of At-Risk Status to Later Violent Behavior

| | *Outcome Status* | | |
	Violent	Not violent	Total
At risk	(Cell A) 7.0%	(Cell B) 18.8%	25.8%
Not at risk	(Cell C) 12.2%	(Cell D) 62.0%	74.2%
Total	19.3%	80.7%	100.0%

figure. The values for cells A through D are aligned from top to bottom near the channels that show the flow from the predictor condition to the outcome. The width of each channel reflects precisely the proportion of individuals present in each condition of the relationship of prior status to later violent behavior. We used SigmaPlot data graphing software to create a scatterplot of the percentage values and then used the software's line-draw function to connect the points.[2] From Figure 9.1 it is easy to evaluate the transitional likelihood of moving from one condition on the previously measured antecedent to another condition on the outcome.

Presenting the Results of Multiple Predictors. A second question when assessing the effectiveness of risk factors for selecting individuals for intervention is, "How do risk factors compare to one another in predicting later violent behavior?" That is, how well does one or a set of risk factors predict violent behavior, relative to other risk factors? One common way of presenting such information is provided in Table 9.2. All the information needed to reconstruct full contingency tables is presented, but the table focuses attention on the true-positive rate (the percentage of those predicted to be violent who were violent) and on the false-negative rate (the percentage of those not predicted to be violent who were later violent).

While these cells are useful for describing the conditionality of causation, they are not necessarily useful for choosing which predictor is likely to be best for selecting cases for intervention. This choice depends on what selection error or errors intervention planners are trying to minimize. For example, Table 9.2 does not give the false-positive rate, a crucial value when there are potential negative consequences of being selected for intervention. Nor is it easy to determine the sensitivity of each predictor. Sensitivity indexes the proportion of individuals positively identified by the predictor who later display the out-

Figure 9.1. Graph of the Data in Table 9.1

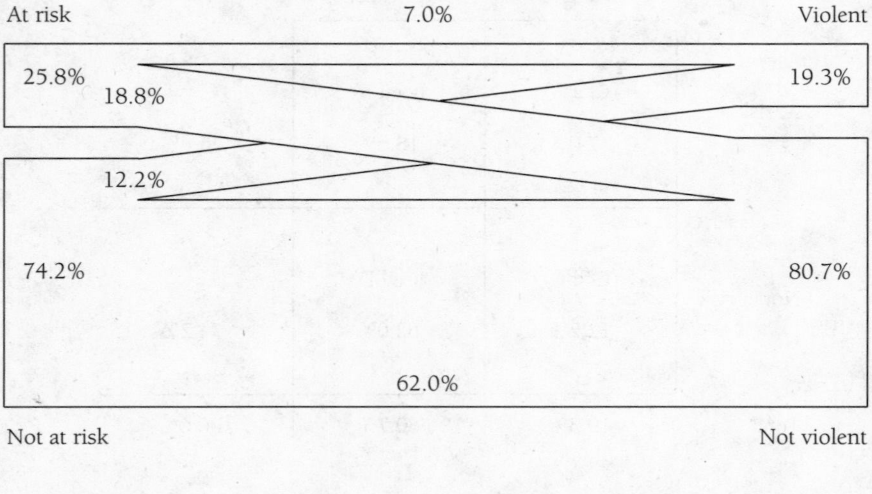

come. Since individuals deemed to be at risk by their status on a predictor are
candidates for intervention, sensitivity is useful for estimating, in advance, the
maximum potential impact of an intervention. Neither of these values are presented in Table 9.1, although they can be calculated from the data.

Conclusion

An alternative display that presents all the data of the two-by-two table and
makes comparisons of the performance of predictors much more salient can
be found in Figure 9.2. Each bar in this figure contains all the data of a two-
by-two contingency table, in percentages. The total height of the bar above
the 0 line represents the average percentage of the distribution that was positively identified by the predictor construct. The depth of the bar below the
0 line represents the percentage of the distribution that was negatively identified by the predictor construct. The gray bar above the 0 line represents the

Table 9.2. Table with Synthesized Predictor Contingency Data

Predictor Construct[a]	Number Predicted[b]	Percent Violent[c]	Mean Correlation[d]
All predictors			0.12
At risk	65	27.1	
Not at risk	186	16.4	
Aggressive behavior			0.18
At risk	59	32.2	
Not at risk	161	15.3	
Other personal characteristics			0.10
At risk	84	24.9	
Not at risk	166	16.4	
Family experiences			0.11
At risk	53	27.8	
Not at risk	197	17.0	
School, social, and SES experiences			0.10
At risk	79	24.9	
Not at risk	171	16.5	

Data calculated from mean correlations, mean within construct selection rates, and grand mean violence base rate

[a] Number of correlations contributing to findings: all predictors, 482; aggressive behavior, 139; other
personal characteristics, 128; family experiences, 104; school, social, and socioeconomic experiences,
111

[b] Calculated number based on a hypothetical sample of 250 cases

[c] Percentage of those at risk and not at risk exhibiting later violence

[d] Sample size weighted mean correlation

average percentage of true positives, while the gray bar below the 0 line represents the average percent of false negatives. The total length of the gray bar represents the best estimate from these data of the mean base rate of violent behavior in a normal population. The white bar above the 0 line represents the percentage of false positives, while the white bar below the 0 line represents the percentage of true negatives in these data. Figure 9.2 was generated by superimposing four bar plots (one plot for each cell in the five two-by-two tables represented) on a single graph using SigmaPlot data graphing software. From Figure 9.2 it is much easier to compare the values and ratios that were available from Table 9.2 across the four constructs and to make judgments of the relative usefulness of these different predictors for selecting cases for intervention.

Figure 9.2. Graph of the Data in Table 9.2

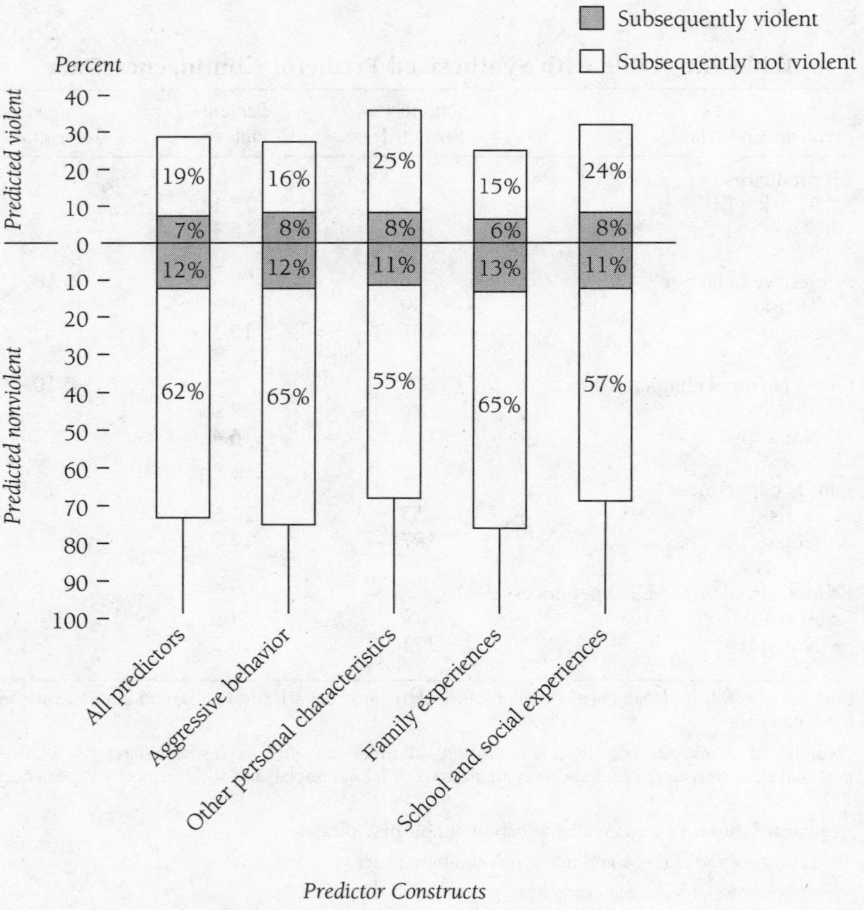

In experimental settings, subjects tend to commit various errors when making judgments based on contingency data (see, for example, Dawes, 1988; Hogarth, 1987; Kahneman, Slovic, and Tversky, 1982). To reduce the likelihood that these types of errors are carried into the field by those using research findings to select cases for intervention, it is essential that evaluators present results that are not only easy to interpret but also difficult to misinterpret. Visually graphing all the relevant data from two-by-two tables is one method for increasing the usefulness of research findings for program planners while reducing the likelihood that those findings will be used to draw inappropriate conclusions due to misinterpretation.

Notes

1. The data for this example come from a meta-analysis of sixty-eight prospective longitudinal studies. From these studies, 998 correlations representing the empirical relationship of ninety-three predictor constructs with some form of later violent behavior were extracted (Derzon, 1996). In the current analysis, multiple measures of similar prospective relationships based on the same samples measured at the same times were averaged. Thus, each subject sample contributed only one correlation to an estimate of the relationship between a prospective measure and later violent behavior. This averaging reduced the 998 correlations to 482 mean estimates. These were then sorted into four "piles" representing the relationship of prior aggressive behaviors, other personal characteristics, family experiences, and school, social, and socioeconomic experience with some form of later violent behavior. For each of these four predictor constructs, its sample size–weighted mean correlation with later violent behavior was then calculated.

The next step was to make fullest use of the data to estimate the cell values of the hypothetical two-by-two table, whose *phi* would be the mean correlation of each of the four relationships. This was done by solving a set of simultaneous equations using the four mean correlations and best estimates of the predictor and outcome marginals. Of the 482 correlations, 255 contained data for estimating these marginals and were based on normal (not criminal or treatment) populations. The outcome marginals for these 255 correlations were averaged to set the outcome marginal across all predictor constructs. Since each predictor has its own natural rate of occurrence in the population, the marginal for each predictor construct was averaged separately.

2. Each percentage on the y-axis was plotted once at four intervals on the x-axis. To separate the at-risk values from the not-at-risk values and the violent from the nonviolent percentages, ten "percentage" points were added to the at-risk and violent values.

References

Dawes, R. *Rational Choice in an Uncertain World.* Orlando: Harcourt Brace, 1988.
Derzon, J. H. "A Meta-analysis of the Efficacy of Various Antecedent Behaviors, Characteristics, and Experiences for Predicting Later Violent Behavior." *Dissertation Abstracts International,* 1996, 57, 748. (University Microfilms No. 9617437.)
Einhorn, H. J., and Hogarth, R. M. "Judging Probable Cause." *Psychological Bulletin,* 1986, 99, 3–19.
Hogarth, R. *Judgement and Choice: The Psychology of Decision.* New York: Wiley, 1987.
Kahneman, D., Slovic, P., and Tversky, A. *Judgments Under Uncertainty: Heuristics and Biases.* Cambridge, England: Cambridge University Press, 1982.
McNemar, Q. *Psychological Statistics.* (3rd ed.) New York: Wiley, 1966.

JAMES H. DERZON *is research associate at the Center for Crime and Justice Policy, Vanderbilt Institute for Public Policy Studies, Nashville, Tennessee.*

A scatterplot graph proves effective for representing data from a pooled time series.

Graphing Impact from Pooled Time Series: School Districts' Energy Savings in Arizona

Lois W. Sayrs

The Arizona legislature enacted a special budget provision allowing Arizona school districts to purchase energy-saving devices and services in excess of their revenue-control limit. Before this provision was slated to expire in June 1995, the legislature asked the state auditor general to determine whether anticipated reductions in utility expenditures had actually been realized in the school districts. Our results would be used to help legislators decide whether to continue the budget provision or let it lapse.

We developed a quasi-experimental design to evaluate the energy savings program. We compared preprogram energy consumption to postprogram energy consumption, as measured in kilowatt hours from monthly utility bills. Only 20 of a possible 226 school districts in Arizona participated in the energy-savings program, and only 15 had programs in place for six months, the time frame needed to yield comparison data. All fifteen districts instituted energy-savings programs independently of each other, using a variety of contractors to achieve various outcomes. Each project was completed at different times.

Six of the fifteen eligible districts were selected nonrandomly. We chose one district with a project that we classified as large in scope, virtually a reconstruction of the entire district's energy system. Two were classified as moderate in scope. Moderate-scope projects included some capital improvements to

The author wishes to thank the Arizona Office of the Auditor General for generous support in the development of this case example, and in particular Mike Aken, John Hines, Connor Leary, and William Shepard.

decrease energy usage (for example, lower ceilings, automatic light switches) and the installation of temperature controls on the heating and cooling system. Three projects were classified as small in scope, because the district purchased new temperature controls.

Of the six districts, two were urban and four were rural. The six districts represented both the northern and southern Arizona climates. Only two of the districts had used the same contractor, and all six had instituted different projects. One district, for example, switched from electric to gas heat, while another integrated a completely computerized system of building temperature management. A third converted to a more efficient air conditioning system. The cases, though not a random sample, illustrated as representatively as possible how school districts were participating in the energy-savings program. Overall, the study included almost five years (four years preprogram and six to twelve months postprogram) of monthly energy consumption for eighteen schools in six Arizona school districts.

In addition to graphs showing district-level energy consumption patterns for the five-year period, we decided to create a graph that would summarize the data of all six districts. We hoped the second graph would help the legislature evaluate the effectiveness of the program and develop recommendations. Since we had school-level monthly energy consumption data over almost a five-year time span for eighteen schools in six districts, we chose to pool monthly energy consumption data by school and compare preproject expenditures with postproject expenditures for each school-month.[1]

To make the comparison, we collapsed the data down to a single monthly point per school by subtracting preintervention data from postintervention data. One data point represented one month of energy consumption postprogram, minus the average of that month's energy consumption in each of the four years prior to the program. After cleaning the data for missing values and other anomalies, we had 120 data points. The use of schools by months for the six districts would allow us to maximize the sample size.

Original Graphs

The first graphs of the pooled data plotted the difference between preprogram and postprogram average kilowatt hours (kWh) for each school-month of data (see Figures 10.1 and 10.2). All graphs were created using Harvard Graphics. The early graphs used bars or points to represent differences in kWh. We controlled for project scope by placing the schools into two groups, with a unique icon representing scope (small versus moderate and large).

The graphs had many advantages. Namely, they showed how many schools had achieved almost no savings or even increased their kWh usage after participating in the program. We could also easily control for district, scope, contractor, or any other information we had on the projects by using different icons. However, we could not control for more than one variable at a time, because it made the graph too difficult to read. While the graph clearly

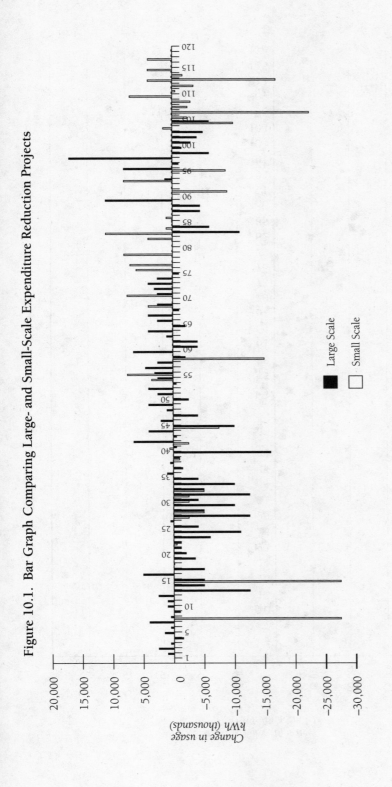

Figure 10.1. Bar Graph Comparing Large- and Small-Scale Expenditure Reduction Projects

Figure 10.2. Dot Graph Comparing Large- and Small-Scale Expenditure Reduction Projects

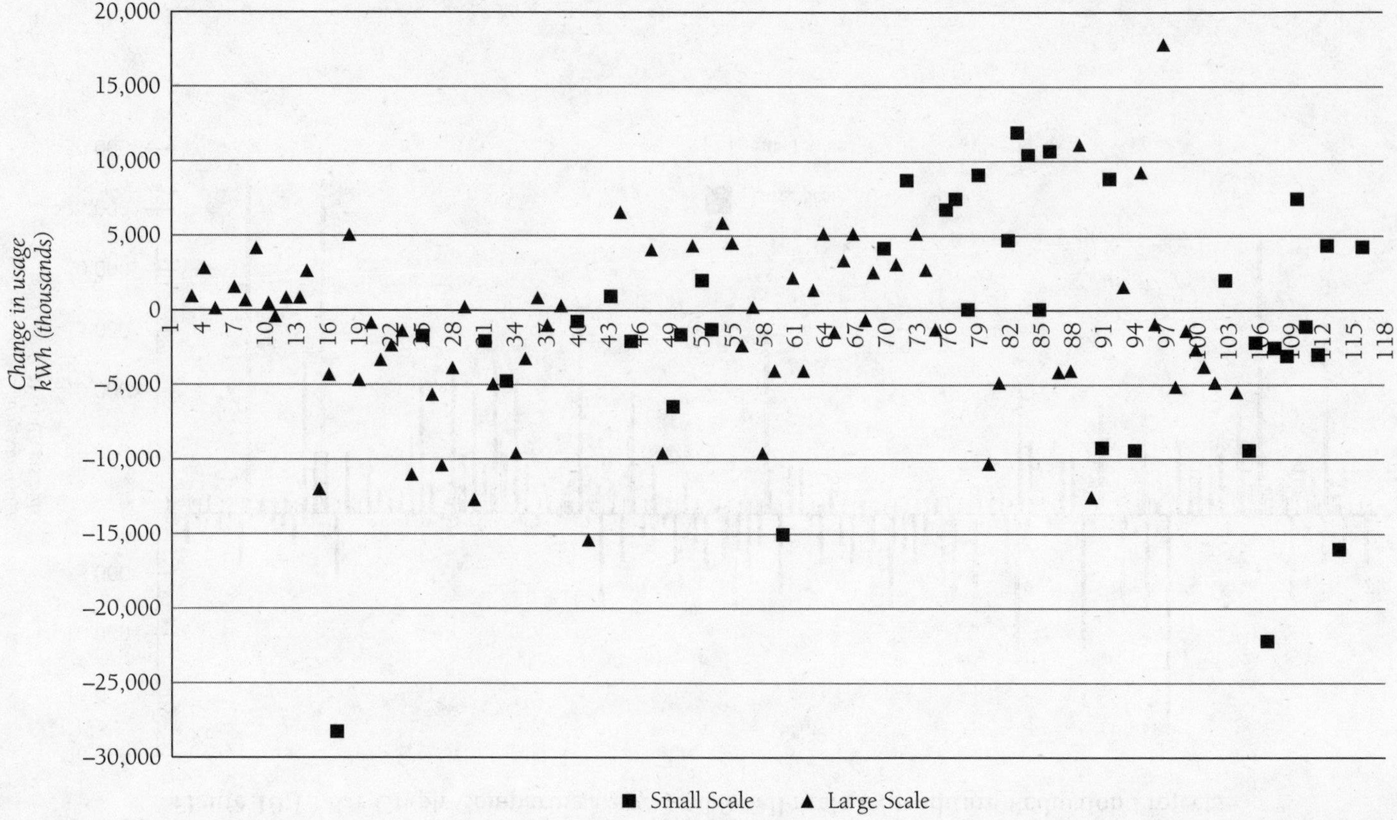

Change in usage
kWh (thousands)

■ Small Scale   ▲ Large Scale

showed that the projects were not paying for themselves, the reader could not assess the magnitude of the original expenditures, only how much the expenditures had changed. A school that had saved 20,000 kWh but had averaged 40,000 kWh per month before participating in the program would look the same as a school that had averaged 80,000 kWh before the program and used 60,000 kWh after the program (also a savings of 20,000 kWh). Standardizing by percentage differences made the comparison even less clear. There was still no clearly interpretable scale. Although the cases were standardized, it remained unclear what a 50 percent increase in usage meant. We were afraid that contractors might claim that we were comparing apples and oranges if we did not standardize, but standardization meant that the reader lost the intrinsic scale. The graphs needed a scale that could easily show the reader where a school was before and where it moved to after participating in the energy-savings program. We also needed to show the reader relative gains and losses in efficiency from preprogram to postprogram.

Revised Graph

Because of these concerns with the original graphs, we chose to create a scatterplot (see Figure 10.3). A scatterplot is an analytical device that shows the relationship between two variables. Each case was plotted at the intersection of two data points: the preprogram average and the postprogram point. One axis represented average energy expenditures for that month in kWh before the project, and the other axis represented expenditures for that same month in kWh after the project.

We decided to provide a rough conversion of kWh to dollars but not to use dollars as the scale, since dollars might raise additional questions from the reader (for example, Were only energy expenditures included in the dollar figure we used? What kinds of energy expenditures were used in the calculation? and so on). Kilowatt hours clearly referred to electricity and showed how much was saved, but by providing a conversion of kWh to dollars, the reader could draw his or her own conclusions.

The key to the scatterplot was the diagonal line drawn at a 45-degree angle, which represented no energy savings. The x-axis was labeled "post," and the y-axis was labeled "pre." In standard practice, the x-axis would be "preprogram" and the y-axis would be "postprogram." However, we believed our audience would find it easier to understand the graph with these axes reversed. Any school-months that fell above the 45-degree line represented a savings. Any school-months that fell below it represented a greater expenditure of energy after the energy-saving project was installed than before. The graph was able to show outliers, clusters, and deviations from a neutral point (that is, no gain and no loss). However, the neutral point was not neutral, because the program was designed to save money. Thus, if districts used the same amount of energy before the project as they did after the project, the project would be considered unsuccessful. We plotted only icons that represented project scope to determine whether project scope influenced impact—that is, whether districts that invested more money in the energy savings program realized greater savings. (Indeed, we controlled for other effects too, such as district and contractor. However, these variables had no effect, and we were hesitant to clutter up an already busy graph.)

The revised graph allowed the reader to view directly the energy savings of schools that participated in the program. It clearly showed a cluster around the 45-degree line, suggesting a common savings pattern. So, even without controlling directly for scope, district, or contractor, we were able to show that these variables did not matter. The graph effectively summarized the school-level data and accurately reflected how much data we actually used to draw our conclusions on impact. We could have simply reported the average savings in a table or text; however, the graph provided a more definitive picture of the program's impact.

Figure 10.3. Scatterplot Graph Comparing Large- and Small-Scale Expenditure Reduction Projects

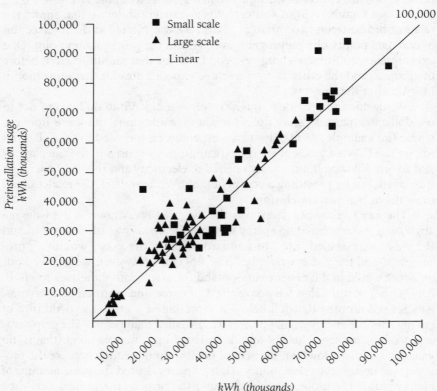

The graph also permitted the reader to quickly reach the conclusion that project scope does not seem to affect savings. In short, greater investments in the energy savings program did not yield greater savings. Projects typically save about 2,000 kWh, or approximately $2,200 per month, regardless of how much was invested. We concluded that the average monthly savings were sufficient to warrant modest investments in energy savings but not large, wholesale renovations. Projects costing $200,000 were saving energy at the same rate as smaller, $20,000 projects.

Impact of the Graph

Our report, which included the revised graph, was presented to the Arizona legislature. As part of the team responsible for the report, I testified on the data collection, research methods, and conclusions from the study. Although the first graph in the report plotted each district's monthly energy expenditures (in kWh) from four years preprogram to a minimum of six months postprogram, the legislature did not refer to those time series graphs in any of their questions to us. Perhaps the graphs were clear and needed no explanation. Or, perhaps the case study method limited the time series graphs' usefulness to the legislators.

I spent most of my time at the podium answering questions about the scatterplot. Legislators were very pleased with the scatterplot because it effectively summarized the most important information. One legislator asked the proverbial $64 question: "So, this graph shows there is no impact?" Ironically, the more traditional presentation of impact in the first time series graph better permitted the legislators to draw the conclusion, albeit limited to a few cases, that the program had not had the anticipated impact. However, they saw it more definitively in the scatterplot of school-months, perhaps because of the number of data points. The scatterplot did not allow us to generalize across the state the way that a statistically representative sample would have. Nowhere in the report or during my testimony did I state that the sample was representative, but I was queried by one legislator on just that point. I told the legislators that the sample was not representative, but the cases did illustrate the types of energy-saving projects around the state.

Although most schools, whether we included them in our evaluation or not, realized that purported savings were chimerical, a few school districts still insisted that, despite our conclusions, they were saving energy and money. Ironically, one of the program's most vehement defenders was a school district that we had included in our review by chance and found to be one of the biggest losers in terms of energy savings. Surprisingly, contractors, some of which were quite large corporations, were not at all critical of our findings.

The legislature, after some debate, decided to allow the budget provision that permitted school districts to budget for energy-saving devices and services to lapse in 1995. Districts could still upgrade energy equipment and purchase services, but only as maintenance, operations, or capital improvements and not in a separate budget category defined as "energy-saving devices and services." Districts would not be able to exceed their budgets to purchase these devices by calculating anticipated savings. We also succeeded in informing the consumers (school districts) that the contractors were prone to calculating cost savings based on a hypothetical baseline instead of documented energy expenditures. In that regard, the report not only answered the questions posed by the legislature and pointed to some potential recommendations but also provided a valuable consumer protection service for school districts purchasing energy-saving devices and services as a "pay-for-itself" investment.

Notes

1. Because we generated a monthly consumption level for each school for each month, the resulting unit of analysis was a school-month. One school, for example, might have sixty months of consumption data, another fifty-four. When all these months of data are pooled into the same database, the total number of cases is well over eight hundred.

LOIS W. SAYRS is senior methodologist at the Arizona Office of the Auditor General.

One difficulty in presenting analyses of complex social networks is how to highlight key elements. This chapter presents a solution that highlights aspects of network structure without distorting or diminishing essential information about the networks.

Shaping Visual Representations of Interorganizational Networks to Tell a Story

Matthew C. Johnsen, Barbara E. Starrett

Interorganizational network analysis provides a framework for evaluators and researchers to measure patterns of interactions within human service systems. Once analysis has determined the key elements in a network structure, the difficulty remains of how to accurately present the findings and highlight the key elements. From the perspective of developing effective visual representations, the challenge is to represent complicated networks in ways that engage readers while leading them to conclusions about network structure. Since the person who creates a graph cannot always be there to interpret it, he or she must create a graph that will be meaningful to readers. Individuals who might be otherwise interested in results of network analyses may be left believing that network representations are simply too complex and not worth the time and effort to study. This chapter discusses the difficulties associated with developing more readily comprehensible visual representations of complex networks. It proposes a solution to these difficulties, aimed at organizing such representations to highlight certain aspects of networks without distorting or diminishing essential information about them.

The authors contributed equally to the development of this chapter, which was presented as a paper at the annual meeting of the Southern Sociological Society, Richmond, Virginia, April 12–14, 1996. The research for this chapter was supported by a grant from the National Institute for Mental Health (MH51410) to the University of North Carolina, Chapel Hill–Duke University Program on Services Research for People with Severe Mental Disorders. The authors acknowledge the suggestions of John Bolland of the Institute for Social Science Research from the University of Alabama.

As an example, the chapter uses data from a study of a human service delivery network in a rural county. The study aimed at understanding systems of care available to persons with serious mental disorders in rural areas. To collect information, agency representatives from forty-two separate programs and agencies were interviewed to gain an understanding of their agency's relationships with one another. The relationship of interest is the strength of information exchange between each pair of agencies. Respondents reported the frequency of these exchanges on a scale ranging from 0 (no exchange) to 4 (a lot of exchange).

Relational data are often presented in two-way matrices known as sociomatrices. The two dimensions of a sociomatrix are indexed by sending actions (rows) and receiving actions (columns). In a single relation network, the sociomatrix is square. After transforming these data from all respondents into a square matrix (of dimensions 42 × 42), the values in the matrix cells were transformed, so that strong ties (2 or greater) were represented by a 1 in the appropriate cells, and weaker ties (less than 2) were represented as 0s. Both solutions presented use the data in this transformed form.

To further assist in the presentation of the data, several additional analyses were performed. To evaluate the cohesive structures within the interorganizational network, k-core analyses were performed. This technique allows researchers to identify tightly connected agencies, which form the innermost core of the network, and less tightly connected agencies, which form the periphery. Information about centrality, which can be used to evaluate the relative importance or prominence of agencies within the network, was also used.

We present two solutions to the problem of creating digraphs of the interagency network. The first solution, which is commonly used (Borgatti, Everett, and Freeman, 1992), uses multidimensional scaling to establish the location of organizations within network space. The second proposes an alternative approach that uses both information about ties between organizations and a priori understanding about network structures to organize the graph in a more readily comprehensible way.

Network Representation Using Multidimensional Scaling

In the first approach, the network is presented using multidimensional scaling (MDS) (Kruskal and Wish, 1978) to locate organizations within network space. This technique uses proximities among organizations as the input. A proximity is a number that indicates how similar or different two organizations are in their patterns of relationships with other organizations. The chief output of the technique is a spatial representation, consisting of a geometric configuration of points, as on a map. Each point in the configuration corresponds to one of the organizations. The configuration reveals the structure in the data, and it often makes the data more easy to understand. The multidimensional scaling approach tends to locate related organizations together, and it also tends to locate highly central actors within the network near the graph's center.

To create a graph using MDS as its organizational basis, we used network analysis software (UCINET 1.4) to create a coordinate map using MDS. The algorithm used is based on the MDS(X) MINISSA program (Borgatti, Everett, and Freeman, 1992). We then loaded network information, including MDS coordinates from UCINET 1.4 to KrackPlot 3.0, a commercially available software program, which allowed us to develop a representation of the network.

While some features of the graph (Figure 11.1) can be appreciated using this technique, several problems persist with the graph. First, it is difficult to interpret. Which agencies are at the center and whether the location of agencies imparts any information remains unclear. In this graph, mental health agencies are identified by a special shape, but the sizing of indicators for agencies makes it difficult to appreciate the relative importance of agencies without counting the ties between agencies.

A second set of problems come from the characteristics of the program itself: MDS solutions are not unique but are subject to local convergence to local minima. Two coordinate maps that represent equally good mathematical solutions may place points in radically different locations. In addition, sometimes the algorithm fails to find the most appropriate configuration.

This approach also fails to incorporate all available information into the solution. Some features of the network structure may be known by researchers through their data collection efforts but do not show up in the graph. For example, it may be clear that some units are subsidiaries of larger units or that certain groups share common membership within interagency councils or coalitions. Procedures such as MDS may or may not illuminate these ties.

Graphically, there are two additional problems that impede immediate understanding of this figure as presented: the size of the symbols for each organization are related to length of the name rather than indicating any particular organizational characteristic, and the concentration of organizations near the center of the graph creates a spaghetti-like tangle of lines, which can make relationships indiscernible.

Revised Graph: Using k-cores to Organize Network Representation

The second solution to the problem, presented in Figure 11.2, uses two network graph properties to organize the graph: k-cores and centrality. K-cores represent one approach to identifying members of cohesive subgroups within networks and can help define the extent to which the relationships within a network of organizations are empirically characterized by zones of activity and which organizations are more or less involved in those exchanges. K-cores may be useful in showing the rough outlines of a network rather than detailed interrelationships between particular network members. They are one of several approaches that can be used to identify members of a network that are particularly well tied to one another or those that are poorly tied to the overall network. Formally, a k-core is a subgraph, in which each node is adjacent to at

Figure 11.1. MDS Graph Depicting Information Exchange Related to Clients with Severe Mental Illness

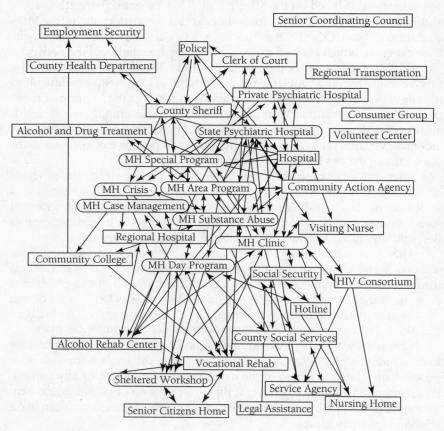

Agency Legend

Alcohol and Drug Treatment

Alcohol Rehabilitation Center

Clerk of Court

Community Action Agency

Community College

Consumer Group

County Health Department

County Sheriff

County Social Services

Employment Security

HIV Consortium

Hospital

Hotline

Legal Assistance

MH Area Program

MH Clinic

MH Day Program

Private Psychiatric Hospital

MH Case Management

MH Crisis

MH Special Program

MH Substance Abuse

Nursing Home

Police

Regional Hospital

Regional Transportation

Senior Citizens Home

Senior Coordinating Council

Service Agency

Sheltered Workshop

Social Security

State Psychiatric Hospital

Visiting Nurse

Vocational Rehabilitation

Volunteer Center

least a minimum number, k, of the other nodes in the subgraph (Wasserman and Faust, 1994). For example, each organization located in a k-core with a k-value of seven will have at least seven ties with other members of that set of organizations. Because k-cores are defined by the minimum number of adjacencies that must be present, they represent areas of a graph where other interesting cohesive subgroups may be found (Seidman, 1983; Johnsen and others, 1996).

Centrality is a measure of the prominence or importance of an organization within a social network. Organizations are considered prominent if the ties of the organization make the organization particularly visible to other organizations in the network. Here the simplest kind of centrality—degree centrality—has been used for illustrative purposes as the basis for organizing this graph. Alternatively, other measures of network centrality (of which there are many, see Wasserman and Faust, 1994) could be employed with similar effectiveness.

In this approach, the network has been organized into three concentric rings of organizational participants. These rings represent the organizations included in the innermost core ($k = 7$), agencies in intermediate cores (the semiperiphery) ($k = 2, 3, 5, 6$), and agencies in the outer cores (the periphery) ($k = 0, 1$). Combined with a legend, which further distinguishes k-core membership, core membership within the graph is more readily interpretable, and the relative connectedness of various agencies (and sectors) is unambiguously acknowledged.

Furthermore, key linkage roles of certain core agencies (most notably, 1, 2, and 3) can be more easily distinguished, because the sizes of symbols representing each agency have been varied to correspond with the relative centrality of each organization within the network. This makes it possible not only to quickly identify the core group of agencies within the network but also to understand which agencies *within* that core are *most* central to the network as a whole. While it would have been possible to create a series of concentric rings (one for each of the k-cores), the solution presented here simplifies understanding the network by organizing agencies into three easily represented (and easily understood) groups: the innermost core, the semiperiphery, and the periphery.

Producing this figure involved several steps. First, we used UCINET to analyze the data, including k-core membership and degree centrality for the network. Second, we used the circle layout format in KrackPlot to produce three different graphs. The first was a circular depiction of only those organizations in the innermost core, the second a circular depiction of organizations in the innermost core and semiperiphery, and the third a circular depiction of all organizations. From these original graphs we used the direct-control positioning function in KrackPlot to produce a new graph with members of all three cores, with positions in the two inner cores from the earlier graphs. When satisfied with positions of all nodes, we exported the graph into a PostScript file. Finally, we used the resulting coordinates to size the tokens according to each organization's degree centrality.

Figure 11.2. Revised Graph, Using *k*-Cores and Centrality

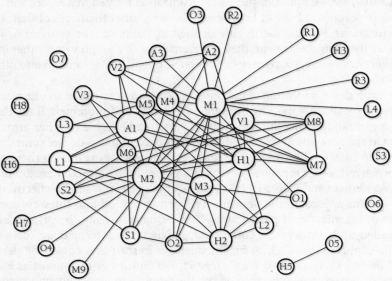

Agency Legend

Sectors
A = Alcohol and Drug Abuse
H = Health Care
L = Law/Judicial
M = Mental Health
O = Other
R = Residential
S = Social Services
V = Vocational Rehabilitation

Innermost Core
(K7)
M1 Mental Health Clinic
M2 Mental Health
   Area Program
A1 Substance Abuse Program
H1 Regional Hospital
M3 Mental Health
   Day Program
V1 Vocational Rehabilitation
M4 Mental Health
   Special Program
M5 Mental Health Crisis
M6 Mental Health
   Case Management

Semiperiphery
(K6)
L1 County Sheriff
H2 Hospital
M7 State Psychiatric
   Hospital
L2 Police
(K5)
V2 Vocational
   Rehabilitation
V3 Sheltered Workshop
A2 Alcohol
   Rehabilitation Center
(K3)
S1 Social Security
M8 Private Psychiatric
   Hospital
S2 County Social
   Services
(K2)
A3 Alcohol and
   Drug Treatment
L3 Clerk of Court
O1 Hotline
O2 Community College

Periphery
(K1)
O3 Service Agency
H3 Visiting Nurse
H4 Regional Hospital
O4 Community Action Agency
O5 HIV Consortium
M9 Private Psychiatric
   Hospital
H5 Visiting Nurse
R1 Senior Citizens
   Home
H6 County Health
   Department
R2 Nursing Home
(K0)
H7 Regional Hospital
R3 Nursing Home
L4 Legal Assistance
O6 Senior Coordination
   Council
S3 Employment Security
H8 Visiting Nurses
O7 Regional Transportation
P8 Volunteer Center

The advantages of this method for representing networks are several. First, the reader can clearly distinguish core and peripheral organizations at a glance and can quickly evaluate the relative importance of organizations within cores, based on their size. Second, this information uses more information known about the network (in this case, k-cores and centrality) as the basis for organizing the network. Third, the critical linkage roles of certain organizations can be readily appreciated.

Conclusion

The strategy for visualizing networks described here is based, to some extent, on Krempel's approach (1993) to more elegant visual representation of networks. The general idea of the proposed method is to begin by placing the most important network elements in the mapping process, not allowing less important network elements to change the graph locations assigned to these more important elements. There are several steps in Krempel's proposed method:

1. Sort all nodes according to their structural importance.
2. For all elements, from most important to least important, do the following:
   a. Evaluate all admissible locations in the model space for their minimal overall distance to those nodes to which there is a link.
   b. Assign the node under consideration to a position in the model space that has not yet been assigned.
   c. Mark the position as being taken.
3. Repeat the steps in 2 above until all elements have been assigned a location.
4. Repeat the entire process several times.

While not fully implementing Krempel's approach, the above example has adapted it to develop a more elegant visual representation of very complex data. In this case, k-cores and centrality were used to determine the most important elements.

It should be noted that while the second representation is an improvement in several respects, it may still be difficult for readers to correctly distinguish the size of the tokens. Henry (1995) discusses the perceptual errors associated with making these distinctions, noting that these errors are somewhat more likely when comparisons are made in terms of area than with simple linear comparisons.

Extensions of this approach involve developing the capability not only to position organizations within networks to display relative centrality but also to use the color or pattern of the figure to represent other important characteristics, such as human services sector membership. This, in combination with the k-core placement, allows readers to quickly distinguish the most central organizations within a core (without having to count ties between agencies) and to appreciate the sectoral membership of the core and periphery. In addition, it may be important for readers to note that the approach described here is equally applicable to representation of other types of social networks, including networks of individuals, industries, or even countries.

While constructing these graphs was time-consuming, we consider the time to have been well spent. When considering the value of time spent, we would do well to heed Henry's advice: "Unless we undertake the process of directly communicating our complex research findings to lay audiences, trusting their intelligence, our work may go underutilized and its value underestimated" (1995, p. 35).

References

Borgatti, S., Everett, M., and Freeman, L. *UCINET IV Version 1.0 Reference Manual.* Columbia, S.C.: Analytic Technologies, 1992.

Henry, G. T. *Graphing Data: Techniques for Display and Analysis.* Thousand Oaks, Calif.: Sage, 1995.

Johnsen, M. C., Morrissey, J. P., Calloway, M. O., Ullman, M., and Starrett, B. E. "Exploring Core and Periphery in Service Delivery Networks for Persons Who Are Homeless and Mentally Ill." Paper presented at Sunbelt XVI: International Sunbelt Social Network Conference, Charleston, S.C., 1996.

Krempel, L. "Simple Representations of Complex Structures: Strategies for Visualizing Network Structure." Paper presented at the Third European Conference for Network Analysis, Munich, 1993.

Kruskal, J. B., and Wish, M. *Multidimensional Scaling.* Thousand Oaks, Calif.: Sage, 1978.

Seidman, S. B. "Network Structure and Minimum Degree." *Social Networks,* 1983, *5,* 269–287.

Wasserman, S., and Faust, K. *Social Network Analysis: Methods and Applications.* Cambridge, England: Cambridge University Press, 1994.

MATTHEW C. JOHNSEN *is research assistant professor in the Department of Psychiatry at the University of North Carolina at Chapel Hill and a research fellow at the Cecil G. Sheps Center for Health Services Research.*

BARBARA E. STARRETT *is a research fellow at the Cecil G. Sheps Center for Health Services Research.*

CONCLUSION: KEYS TO GOOD GRAPHING

If seeing is believing, then the graphs featured in this sourcebook can help make your evaluation findings more believable. Graphs are often a solution to common problems in evaluation. They allow evaluators to communicate specific findings to audiences that may have little time or interest in deciphering a narrative report or a set of tables. Evaluators can communicate more information and to a wider audience through graphs than through tables or text.

The cases in this sourcebook illustrate that there is no magic formula for producing good graphs. It requires ingenuity, yes; and perseverance, certainly; and a critical eye for viewing early drafts, without a doubt. But producing a good graph really follows from adopting a few simple practices and consistently using them when we begin graphing.

Consider Your Skills

Most of us do not try to create a graph on a daily or even weekly basis. Every few months or so, as the need arises, we dust off the graphing software and test our memories. Graphing is a means to a very specific end. But the path to that end can be highly variable. If a particular graphing situation commonly comes up in your work, such as the need to present changes over time, you should jot down the settings used to generate a particular graph on the desk copy of your reports. If, for example, you frequently use one survey question to screen certain respondents and follow-up with an additional question, the format offered by Brown, Marks, and Straw (Chapter Two) should be stored away. If you frequently show the extent to which several units change from one time period to another, Sinacore (Chapter Five) provides a useful display format for these graphs. The point here is that once you have invested the time to add a new format to your repertoire, consistently make the notes that will keep that skill ready. For example, to get you started the second time around you might want to save a copy of the program used in your graphing software files that is labeled by the type of graph.

It is important to acquire the essential technical skills needed to make effective graphs. For example, a simple matter such as suppressing the space between bars on a graph requires knowledge of the appropriate software functions. In addition, you must be able to differentiate which type of graph best serves your purpose. For example, Sinacore illustrates in Chapter Five that a dot graph (which shows change) is far more effective for this purpose than a bar graph, because the bar graph (which shows the pre and post values) leaves a large amount of space empty and doesn't show change from a common scale. For other examples, see the first graphs from Sayrs (Chapter Ten) and Turpin (Chapter Six). Graphing requires a marriage of skill and purpose with an eye towards time, both that of the person doing the graphing and that of the audience.

If you have only limited experience with graphs, start with some basic formats and hone them for your purposes. Perhaps a graph in this sourcebook provides a format that you need for your purposes. You may need to consult some other reference works as well, such as Tufte's *The Visual Display of Quantitative Information* (1983), probably the most cited book in the field, or *Graphical Methods for Data Analysis,* by Chambers, Clevelend, Kleiner, and Tukey (1983), a book of more technical graphs. *Graphing Data* (Henry, 1995) guides the graphing process based on the research and theory of graphical displays. Of course, excursions into the literature and playing with options in your software program to learn how to do the graphs shown in any of the sources will take time, which brings us to the next point.

Allocate Enough Time

Even experienced graph makers take time to produce a good graph. The chapters in this sourcebook are witnesses to the futility of using the default graph. If Turpin (Chapter Six) had used the bar format for her presentations, would the effect of the intervention have been as clear to the audience? Would the downward national trend that caught up with and eventually surpassed the hospital's reduction in patient lengths of stay have been so easily traced? It takes time to make graphs that can effectively communicate information standing alone. The extra days used to improve the quality of the data collected or to clean the data once more will take their toll on the graphing process and communication of results. Shortcuts are essential (such as using one graphing program exclusively and dedicating its most useful formats to memory), but even with shortcuts you will need time. Fortunately, there are other, task-specific shortcuts that you can use. For example, I keep a copy of the codes for my favorite software's specific plot symbols on a yellow sticky note on my monitor. When I am in a hurry, I can never find the codes in the manual.

In addition, you must consider the time that the audience or reader will have to interpret the graph. A succession of quick snapshot overheads for a presentation will involve different audience time than will a series of complicated graphs in a journal article, for example. Tailor the graph, keeping in mind not only the time needed to make it but also the time needed to read and interpret it. The best starting point is to have a clear notion of the purpose of the graph. The ending point should be to check to see if the graph fulfills its original purpose. It is often said that good writing is rewriting. Good graphing is much the same—you must carefully consider both the before and after graphs and determine if the revised graph still fulfills your purpose.

Know the Graph's Purpose

"Pay me now, or pay me later" is the theme for this section. You either think through the purpose of graphing on the front end and follow the straight line that stretches between two points, or you can start jamming with the data and see where you go. You might get to the same place either way, but a little extra time spent up front thinking about what you want to do can save you time in the long run.

The most usual distinction in purpose is that between discovery, which allows viewers to work their way to your conclusions, and simply stating conclusions (Tukey, 1988; Henry, 1995). The graphical route to discovery is, we fear, too little used. Discovery involves using graphs to find previously unknown characteristics or relationships in the data. Graphs can be used to lead an audience to a discovery or to enhance the researcher's own data analysis efforts. Johnsen and Starrett (Chapter Eleven) illustrate the concept of discovery with their revised graph of interorganizational communication networks. The graph shows relationships that cannot be viewed as directly by any other means. The purpose is to probe the data, to check for outliers that might have influenced your conclusions, and to explore the data. The exploratory data analysis techniques proposed by Tukey (1977) are very useful for this. Sayrs's scatterplot (Chapter Ten) of preintervention and postintervention data is a useful way of probing data, especially since she used different icons as symbols for characteristics of the intervention. If one particular type or intervention showed up above or below the 45-degree line, she would have discovered a relationship that needed more analysis. A point to remember here: *discovery* is often a *purpose,* it is not a substitute for knowing your purpose. When you have analyzed the data and know what you would like your audience to find out, you can refine your purpose and get to the graphical solution more quickly—although as Sayrs recounts from her experience in presenting her information to legislators, the graph was more convincing when the audience used it to reach their own conclusions.

Graphs often occupy a middle ground between discovering and communicating findings: they can be used either to check the plausibility of findings or alternative explanations of the findings. Often the former is done by checking for violations of assumptions of statistical properties, such as the violation of a linear relationship in least-squares regression (Cleveland, 1987; Henry, 1995) or checking for outliers. But substantive concerns can also be checked, as Glymph and Henry illustrate in their second graph (Chapter Four).

Most of the graphs shown in this sourcebook are aimed at speeding audience access to data. The audience is expected to use the data either to reason through their own conclusions or to extract the conclusion of the evaluator. Brown, Marks, and Straw (Chapter Two), in their second series of graphs, show a comparison of one region with the nation and the significant differences. Hypothesis tests are one method of coming to conclusions, so the graph leads the audience to notice those differences and their importance quickly. However, the graph presents the magnitude of these differences in the context of other differences by graphing them all on the same scale and with a format that encourages comparison. The conclusions are quickly accessible, but the *judgements* to be made are in the hands of the reader.

Another way to conceptualize the purpose of a graph is to consider the level of the graphical task that we want the audience to accomplish (Wainer, 1992; Henry, 1995). Do we want the reader to read the actual values off the graph, to find a trend or average, or to compare two trends or two groups? DeVeaux and the audience for his report wanted to accomplish the first task, to read the actual values, as quickly and easily as possible, so they preferred his last figure (this volume). We can look past the basic information as we become more and more knowledgeable about the program being evaluated, but the audience may still need the basics. In another illustration of this point, we can refer to the flowchart by Parker and Mortillaro (Chapter Three). The graph that replaced the table provided the seeds of the question "why" because the graph showed "what" so quickly.

While as evaluators we must be certain to cover the basics, graphs should be used to their full potential in making comparisons. One common mistake in graphical design is in trying to accomplish too much with one graph by packing too much information in, so that the graph becomes unintelligible or confusing to the audience. In three examples in this sourcebook, the authors chose to offer two graphs rather than one overburdened graph (Chapters Four, Two, and Six). Supplying two graphs, each serving their purpose well, may be better than trying to do too much with one. Often the best graphs in a situation will serve two purposes, but two compatible purposes. For example, Bonnet's horizontal bar graphs (Chapter One) allow for both a quick read of the data values and speedy comparisons but also enable more probing of the data as time allows.

Know the Audience

Essential to determining the purpose of the graph is knowing the audience to whom it is addressed. Although they dealt with data from multiple states, Glymph and Henry (Chapter Four) tailored their graphs to their audience, citizens and opinion leaders from one particular state. Anticipating the interests of the audience is an important part of the communication process. But it is important to give the audience quick access to as much data as possible.

The graphs Derzon (Chapter Nine) offers to illustrate the accuracy of using risk factors may broach a subject that is too complex for most audiences. False positives and false negatives have important and different consequences. The public and policymakers should be made aware of the judgments involved in using risk factors. Derzon's graphs show the relationships without making the audience learn the terminology. The graphs illustrate the flow from one status to another. If the relationships are important for the audience to grasp, as they are in this case, a clear graph can raise the level of understanding.

Sayrs (Chapter Ten) also takes a risk with her audience. She uses a scatterplot, the most abstract of all graphs, to show data on the success of an energy conservation initiative. By knowing and respecting the abilities of her audience, she received the dividend of good questions and decisions consistent with her findings. Because the graphs provided enough information for the audience to see the effect of the program, even though they included a complex relational graph, her report encountered relatively little opposition.

The important messages to take away from this discussion of audience include covering the basics as well as taking risks by providing complex information in graphical form when it is needed. Two additional factors will also come into play: the medium of presentation and the technology used to make the graph.

Know the Presentation Media

How is the audience going to access the graph? Options are wide. If the graph is to be used in a live presentation, using color overheads, slides, or a projected LCD display from a computer screen, you will want a different format than if it is to be printed and reproduced in black and white. You must also consider that in a live presentation you will be there to explain the graph and answer questions. Conversely, if the graph will be read independently, all questions must be thought through and answers provided with the graph. If the graph is to be printed, consider the effects of multiple photocopying on the distinctions between shaded bars or areas on the graph. For example, Brown, Marks, and Straw (Chapter Two) differentiate sections of their revised pie-and-bar graph by using textural differences instead of shading. Bonnet (Chapter One) uses a combination of shading and texture to differentiate between bars in her graph. All of these factors, as well as the available technology, inform and limit your graphical choices.

Know the Technology

What you see on the computer screen is not what you get on paper. Nothing is more frustrating than to refine a graph to the point of perfection on-screen and then find that it prints out with misaligned labels and shading that make the symbols indistinguishable. Different printers print graphs in different ways, and different software programs operate differently with different printers. You must figure out and note how your software, computer, and printer work together in order to consistently make effective graphs with the least amount of frustration.

Questions to Ask

Once you have the graph in hand, there are a number of questions you must ask regarding its purpose and effectiveness. Go back to your original purpose, and make sure that you have not gone off track. Try to look at the original and revised graphs with fresh eyes. Ask yourself what you see in the graph. Avoid the trap of getting caught up in getting the techniques right instead of communicating the information you want to communicate. For example, if you decide to convert a pie graph to a bar graph for aesthetic purposes, pay attention to any possible changes in the information the graph conveys rather than on the technique used to make the graph. Is the graph conveying the information that you want to convey? Is the level of information appropriate for your audience? Is the graph easily comprehensible? Is size of the effect or relationship in the graph reflective of its actual size?

For good graphing, you must consider the purpose of your graphs, the tools you have at hand, and the principles of graphing. The principals of good graphing include showing the data clearly and without distortion, designing graphs that provide useful information, and encouraging important comparisons (Henry, 1995). Factors that distinguish a good graph from a less effective one include the order of the displays, the proximity of symbols for comparison, scale and labeling in graphs, and ease of information processing.

References

Chambers, J. M., Cleveland, W. S., Kleiner, B., and Tukey, P. A. *Graphical Methods for Data Analysis*. Pacific Grove, Calif.: Brooks/Cole, 1983.

Cleveland, W. S. "Research in Statistical Graphics." *Journal of the American Statistical Association*, 1987, 82 (398), 419–421.

Henry, G. T. *Graphing Data: Techniques for Display and Analysis*. Thousand Oaks, Calif.: Sage, 1995.

Tufte, E. R. *The Visual Display of Quantitative Information*. Cheshire, Conn.: Graphics Press, 1983.

Tukey, J. W. *Exploratory Data Analysis*. Reading, Mass.:Addison-Wesley, 1977.

Tukey, J. W. "Some Graphic and Semigraphic Displays." In W. S. Cleveland (ed.), *The Collected Works of John W. Tukey*. Pacific Grove, Calif.: Brooks/Cole, 1988.

Wainer, H. "Understanding Graphs and Tables." *Educational Researcher*, 1992, 21 (2), 14–23.

GARY T. HENRY *is director of the Applied Research Center and associate professor in the Departments of Public Administration and Political Science in the College of Policy Studies at Georgia State University.*

KATHLEEN DOLAN *is a research assistant in the Applied Research Center and a Ph.D. student in the Department of Sociology at Georgia State University.*

INDEX

Adcock, M. H., 59n
Adobe PageMaker, 34
Aggregate comparisons, 4, 33–40
Aken, M., 85n
American Association of Retired Persons (AARP): awareness study, 19–22; VOTE program, 17–19, 20
Arinder, M. K., 59n
Arizona, school district energy savings, 85–92
Audience, 73, 104–105

Bar graphs: amount of information in, 14–15; of contingency data, 81–82; double, 43–48; flowchart incorporation of, 28, 29; of historical data, 61, 62–63; horizontal, 4, 9–15; linked to pie charts, 4, 18–19, 20; of pooled time series data, 86–87, 89; revising, 20–22; versus control charts, 53–58; versus line graphs, 60–64, 69–74; versus scatterplots, 86–91
Beckford, I. A., 35
Beherens, J. T., 5
Bell Curve, The (Herrnstein and Murray), 39
Bertin, J., 4, 35
Bliersbach, C. M., 58
Bolland, J., 93n
Bonnet, D. G., 4, 104, 105
Books, on graphing, 102
Borgatti, S., 94, 95
Brassard, M., 55
Brown, H., 4, 101, 103, 105

Campbell, D. T., 70
Centrality, 97–99
Chambers, J. M., 43, 102
Change, over time, 43–48, 53–58
Claris McDraw, 64, 67
Cleveland, W. S., 4, 37, 43, 45, 102, 103
Clustered bar graphs, 9–11
Cohorts, breaking data down by, 5, 64–68
Column graphs, 61, 62–63. See also Bar graphs
Comparisons: aggregate, 4, 33–40; clustered bar graphs for, 9–11; over time, 53–58
Compulsory attendance law, 64–68

Computers, 105. See also Software
Contingency data, 4, 77–83; graphs of, 80–82; tables of, 78–80, 81
Control charts: hi-lo, 56–58; versus bar graphs, 53–58; X-bar, 55–56, 58
Cook, T. D., 70
Cooley, W. W., 35
Corcoran, T., 35
Council for School Performance (Georgia), 34, 37, 40

Data: aggregate, 4, 33–40; change in, over time, 43–48, 53–58; cohort, 5, 64–68; contingency, 4, 77–83; ordinal, 11, 12; performance, 33–40, 60–64; rank-ordered, 11, 12; scaled, 11–12, 13; survey, 17–23
Dawes, R., 77, 83
Dearing, B. E., 27
DeCarlo, F., 44, 46
Derzon, J. H., 5, 77, 83n1, 105
DeVeaux, M., 5, 104
Distortion, 19. See also Simpson's paradox
Domvol, 69; revising graphs of data from, 69–74
Dot charts: of pooled time series data, 86, 88–89; versus double bar graphs, 43–48; versus scatterplots, 86–91
Dot graphs. See Dot charts
Double bar graphs, versus dot charts, 43–48
Dropout rates, 64–68

Edlefsen, L. E., 27
Einhorn, H. J., 79
Energy savings, Arizona school district, 85–92
Enrollment changes, 43–48
Everett, M., 94, 95

False negatives, 77, 78, 80
False positives, 5, 77, 78, 82
Faust, K., 97
Finison, K. S., 58
Finison, L. J., 58
Flowcharts, 27–28; incorporating bar graphs, 28, 29; versus tables, 25–27

107

ORDERING INFORMATION

NEW DIRECTIONS FOR EVALUATION is a series of paperback books that presents the latest techniques and procedures for conducting useful evaluation studies of all types of programs. Books in the series are published quarterly in Spring, Summer, Fall, and Winter and are available for purchase by subscription as well as by single copy.

SUBSCRIPTIONS cost $61.00 for individuals (a savings of 24 percent over single-copy prices) and $96.00 for institutions, agencies, and libraries. Please do not send institutional checks for personal subscriptions. Standing orders are accepted. Prices subject to change. (For subscriptions outside of North America, add $7.00 for shipping via surface mail or $25.00 for air mail. Orders *must be prepaid* in U.S. dollars by check drawn on a U.S. bank or charged to VISA, MasterCard, or American Express.)

SINGLE COPIES cost $20.00 plus shipping (see below) when payment accompanies order. California, New Jersey, New York, and Washington, D.C., residents please include appropriate sales tax. Canadian residents add GST and any local taxes. Billed orders will be charged shipping and handling. No billed shipments to post office boxes. (Orders from outside North America *must be prepaid* in U.S. dollars by check drawn on a U.S. bank or charged to VISA, MasterCard, or American Express.)

SHIPPING (SINGLE COPIES ONLY): $20.00 and under, add $3.50; to $50.00, add $4.50; to $75.00, add $5.50; to $100.00, add $6.50; to $150.00, add $7.50; over $150.00, add $8.50.

DISCOUNTS FOR QUANTITY ORDERS are available. Please write to the address below for information.

ALL ORDERS must include either the name of an individual or an official purchase order number. Please submit your order as follows:
    Subscriptions: specify series and year subscription is to begin
    Single copies: include individual title code (such as PE59)

MAIL ALL ORDERS TO:
    Jossey-Bass Publishers
    350 Sansome Street
    San Francisco, California 94104-1342

FOR SUBSCRIPTION SALES OUTSIDE OF THE UNITED STATES, CONTACT
    any international subscription agency or Jossey-Bass directly.

OTHER TITLES AVAILABLE IN THE
NEW DIRECTIONS FOR EVALUATION SERIES
Jennifer C. Greene, Gary T. Henry, Editors-in-Chief

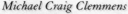